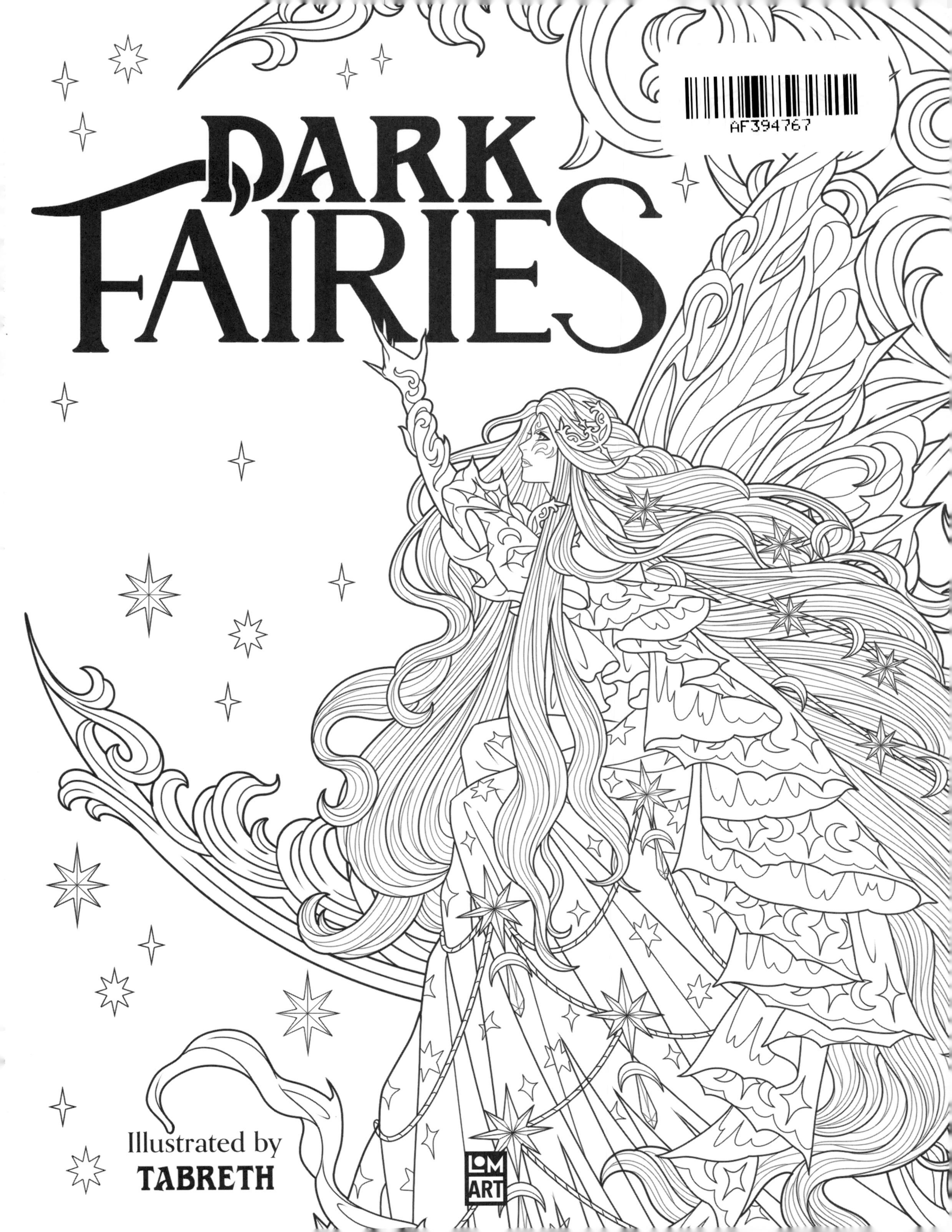

DARK FAIRIES
Illustrated by
TABRETH
LOM ART

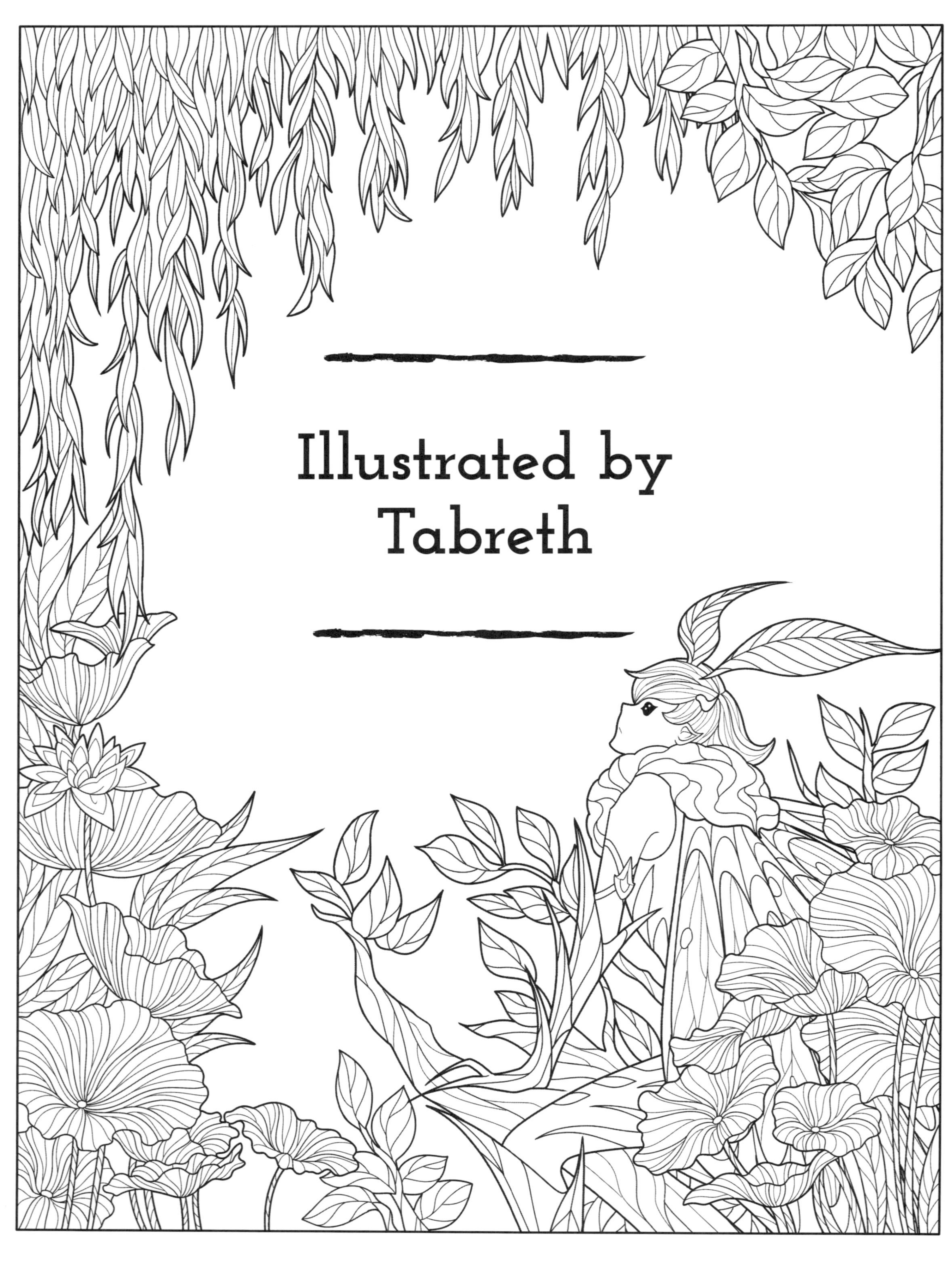
Illustrated by
Tabreth

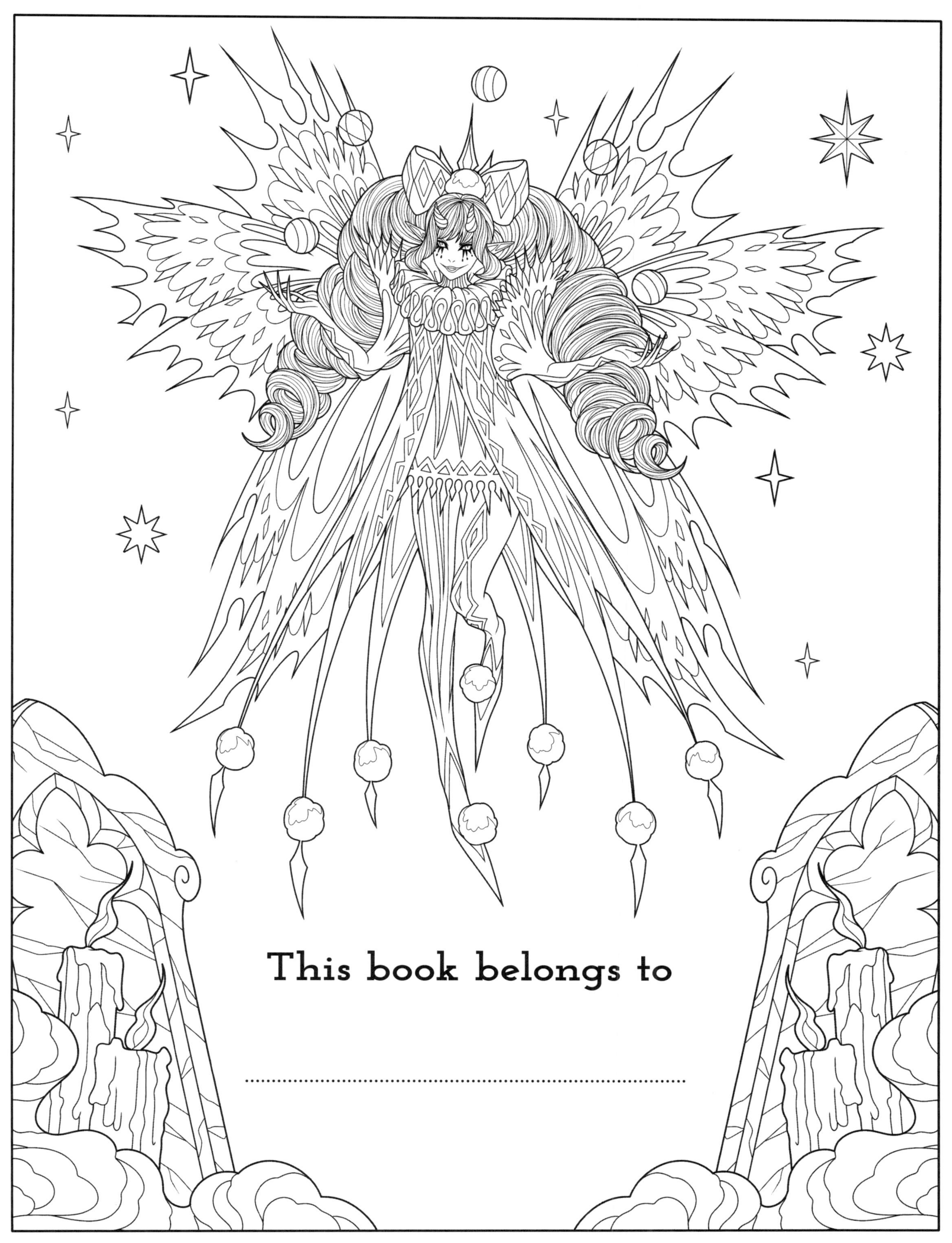

This book belongs to

....

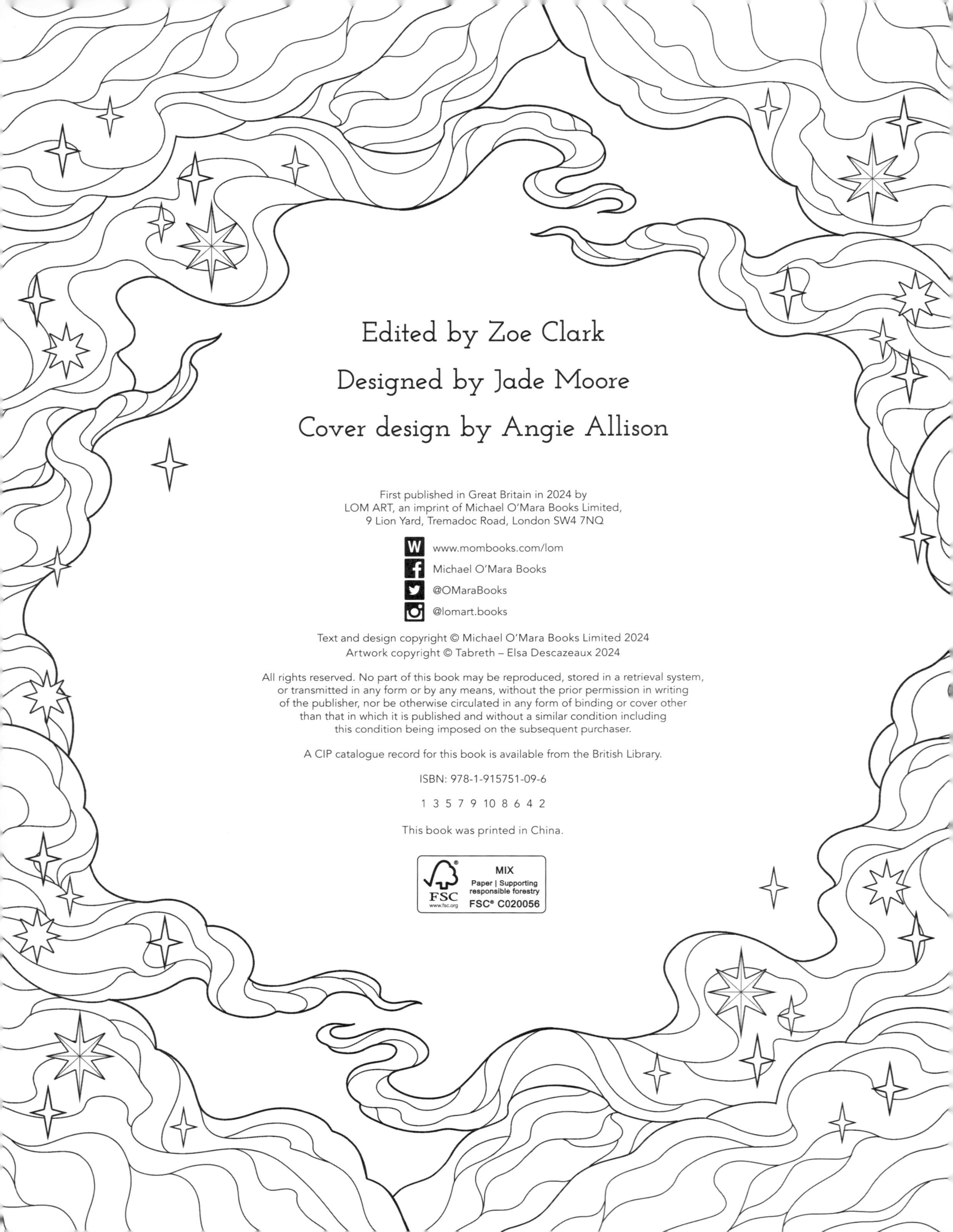

Edited by Zoe Clark

Designed by Jade Moore

Cover design by Angie Allison

First published in Great Britain in 2024 by
LOM ART, an imprint of Michael O'Mara Books Limited,
9 Lion Yard, Tremadoc Road, London SW4 7NQ

www.mombooks.com/lom
Michael O'Mara Books
@OMaraBooks
@lomart.books

A CIP catalogue record for this book is available from the British Library.

ISBN: 978-1-915751-09-6

1 3 5 7 9 10 8 6 4 2

This book was printed in China.

FSC
www.fsc.org

MIX
Paper | Supporting
responsible forestry
FSC® C020056

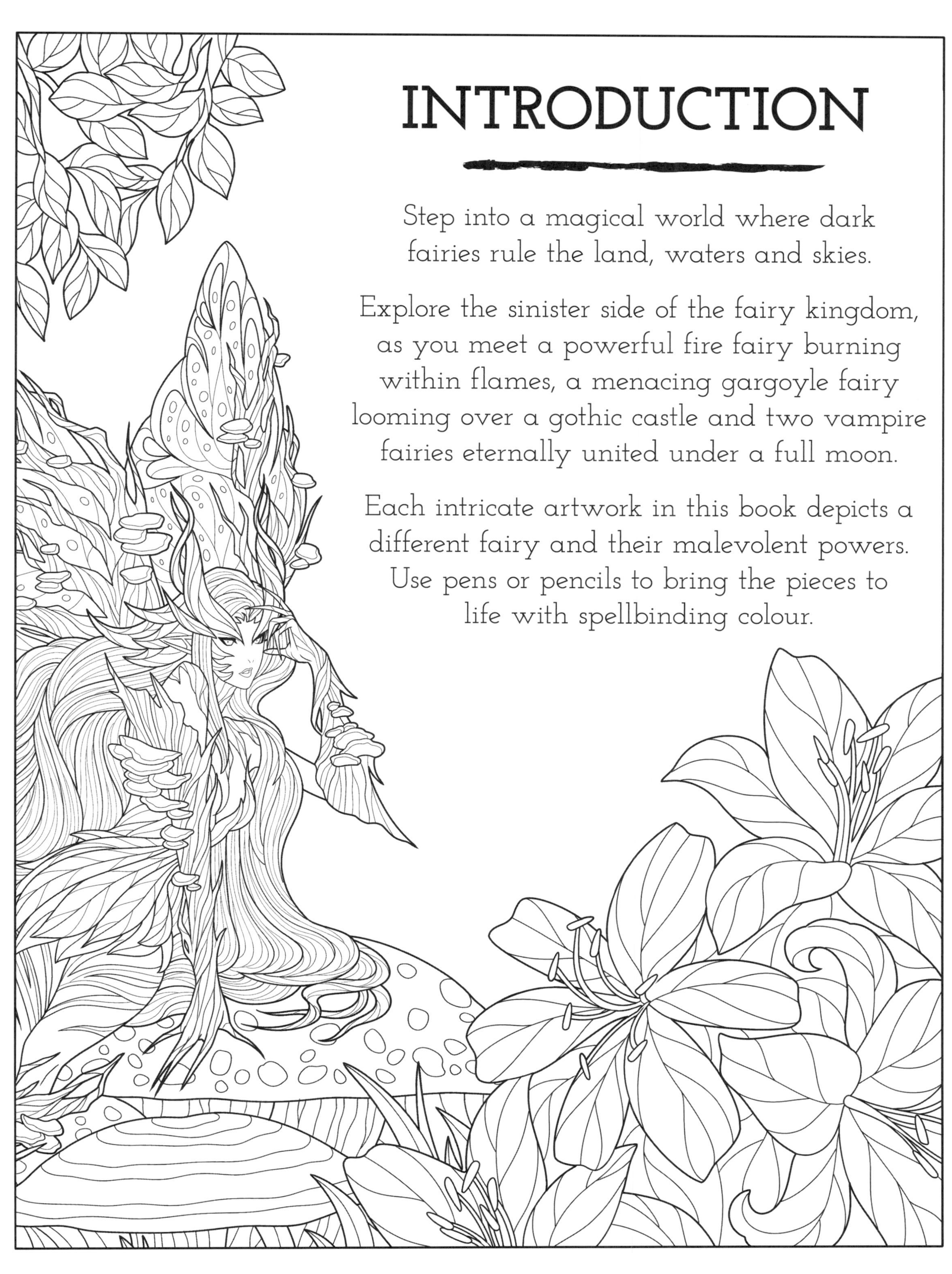

INTRODUCTION

Step into a magical world where dark fairies rule the land, waters and skies.

Explore the sinister side of the fairy kingdom, as you meet a powerful fire fairy burning within flames, a menacing gargoyle fairy looming over a gothic castle and two vampire fairies eternally united under a full moon.

Each intricate artwork in this book depicts a different fairy and their malevolent powers. Use pens or pencils to bring the pieces to life with spellbinding colour.

Moonlight Maiden

Reaching out to the dark side of the moon.

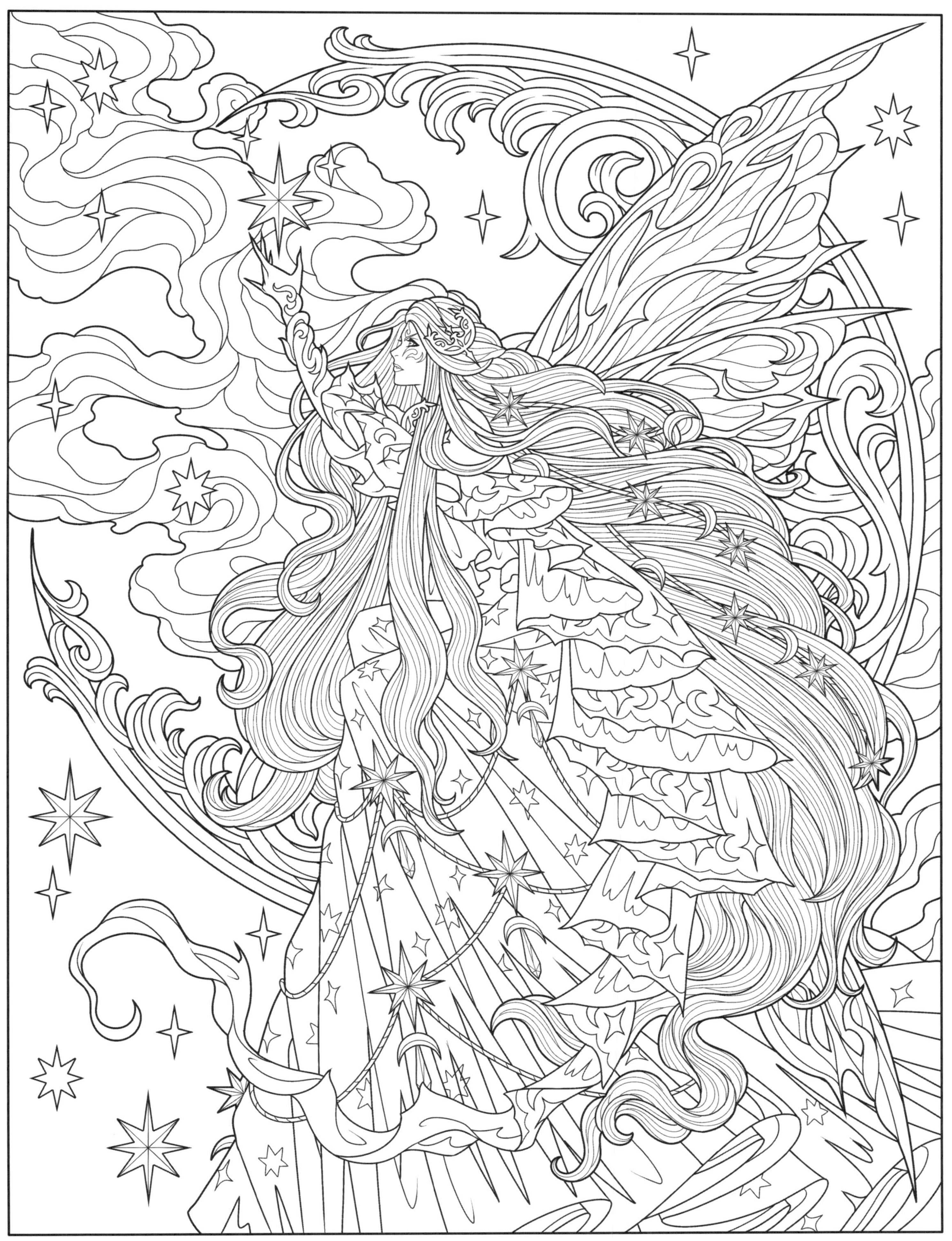

Trick or Treat?

Hauntingly beautiful on Halloween night.

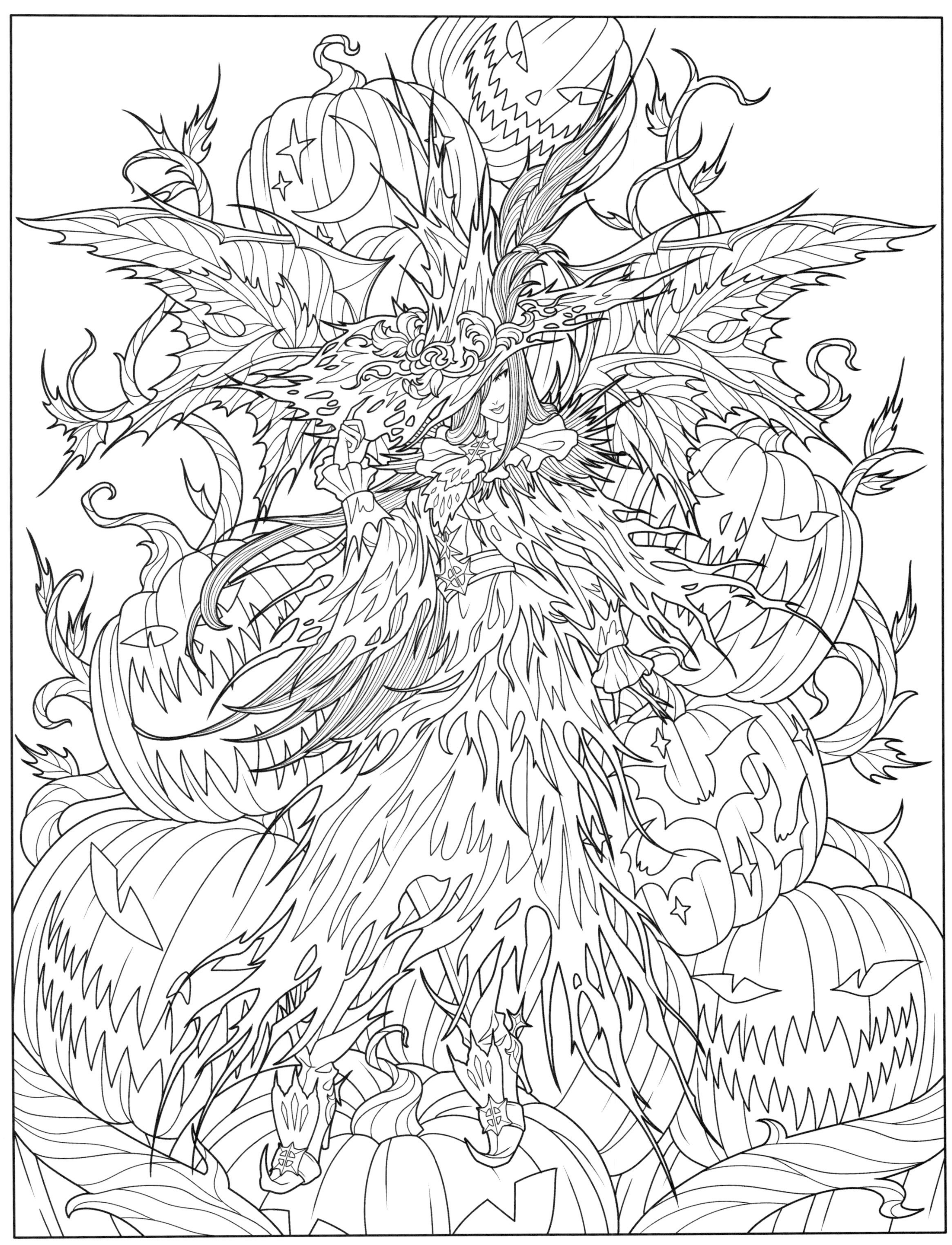

Till Death Do Us Part

A corpse bride longing for her love.

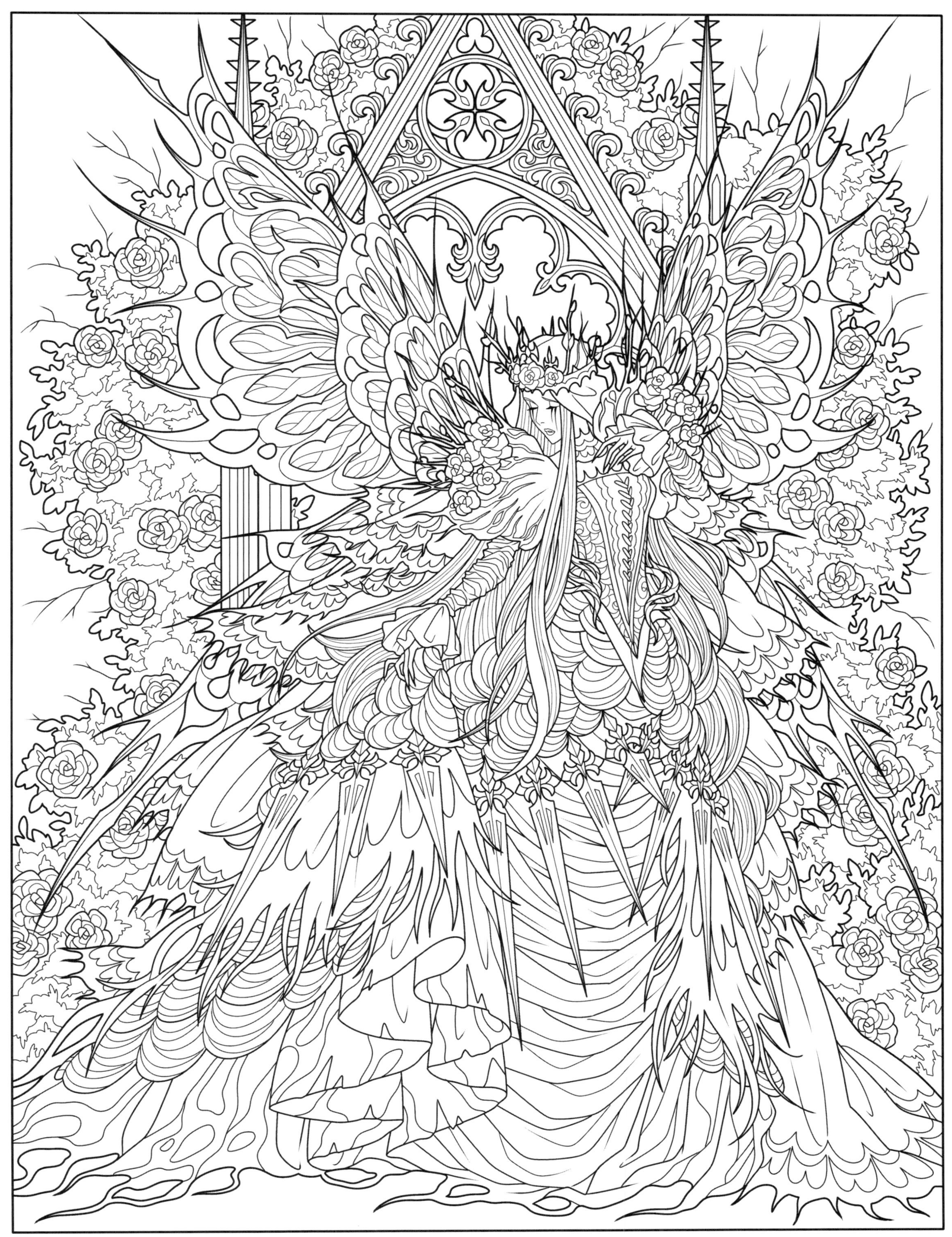

The Druid's Domain

At one with nature in the depths of the ancient forest.

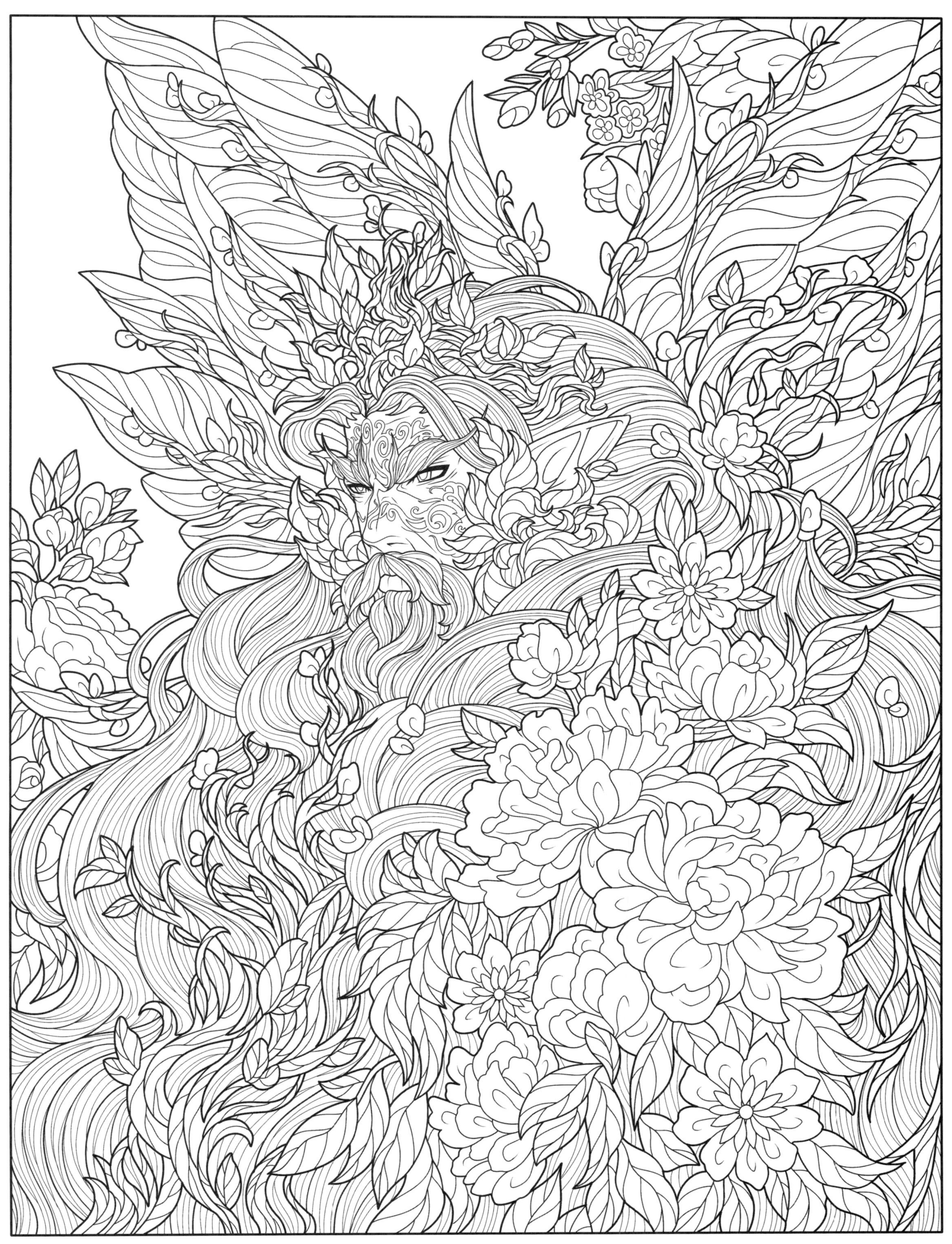

Mirror, Mirror

A wicked queen born of evil and envy.

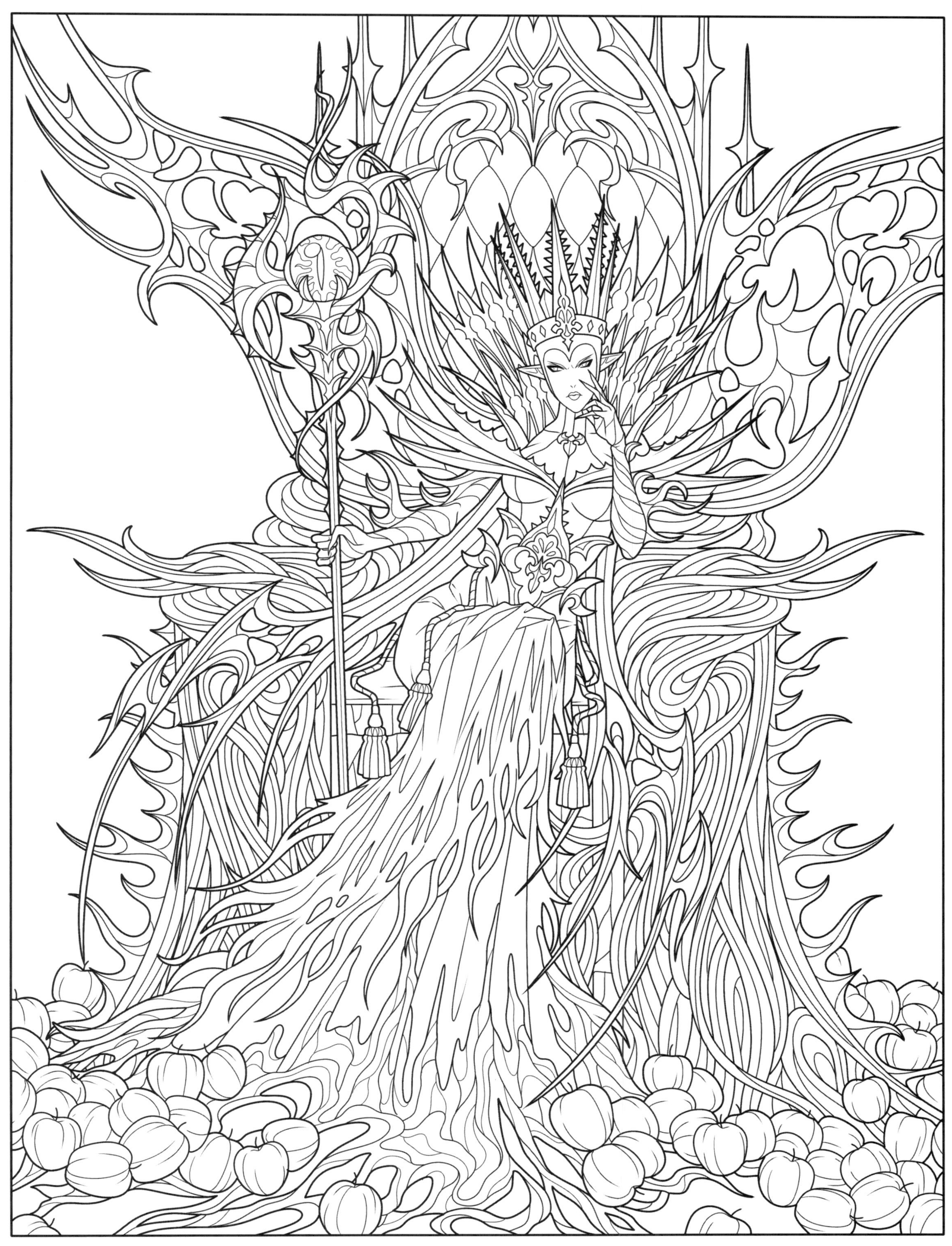

Huntress of the Night

Swift and stealthy as a sharp-eyed owl.

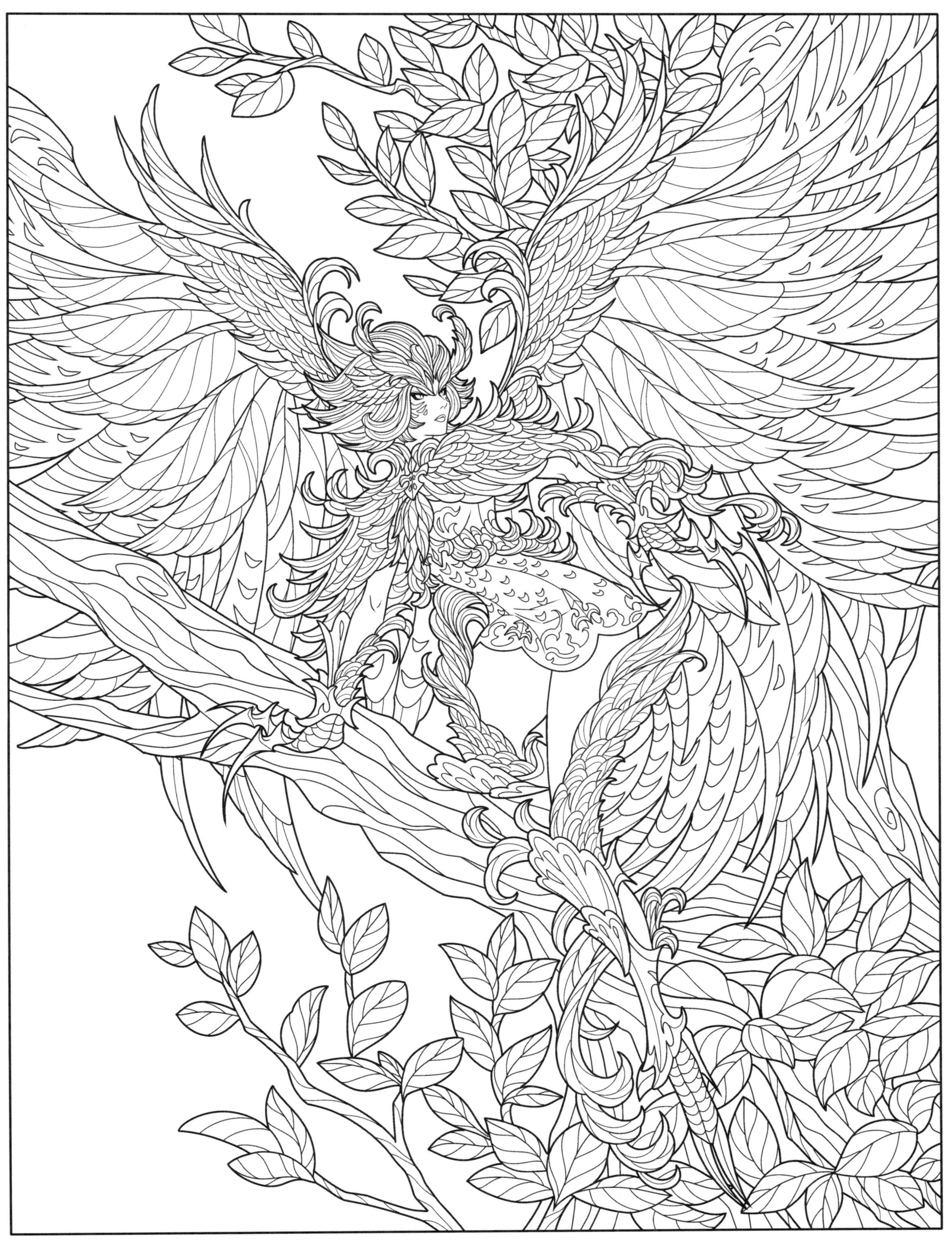

The Warrior's Arrow

Taking deadly aim with masterful precision.

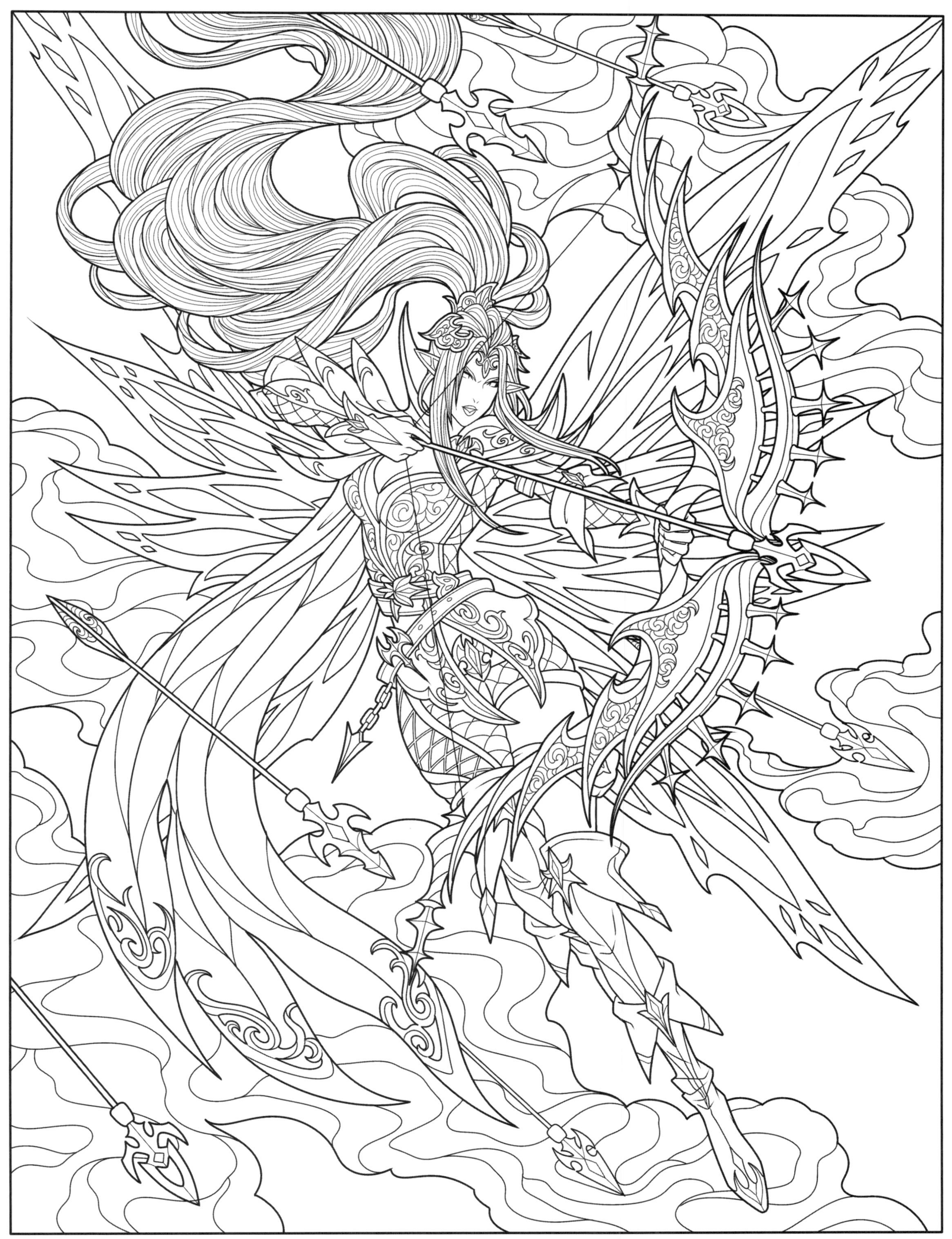

The Nightmare of the Reaper

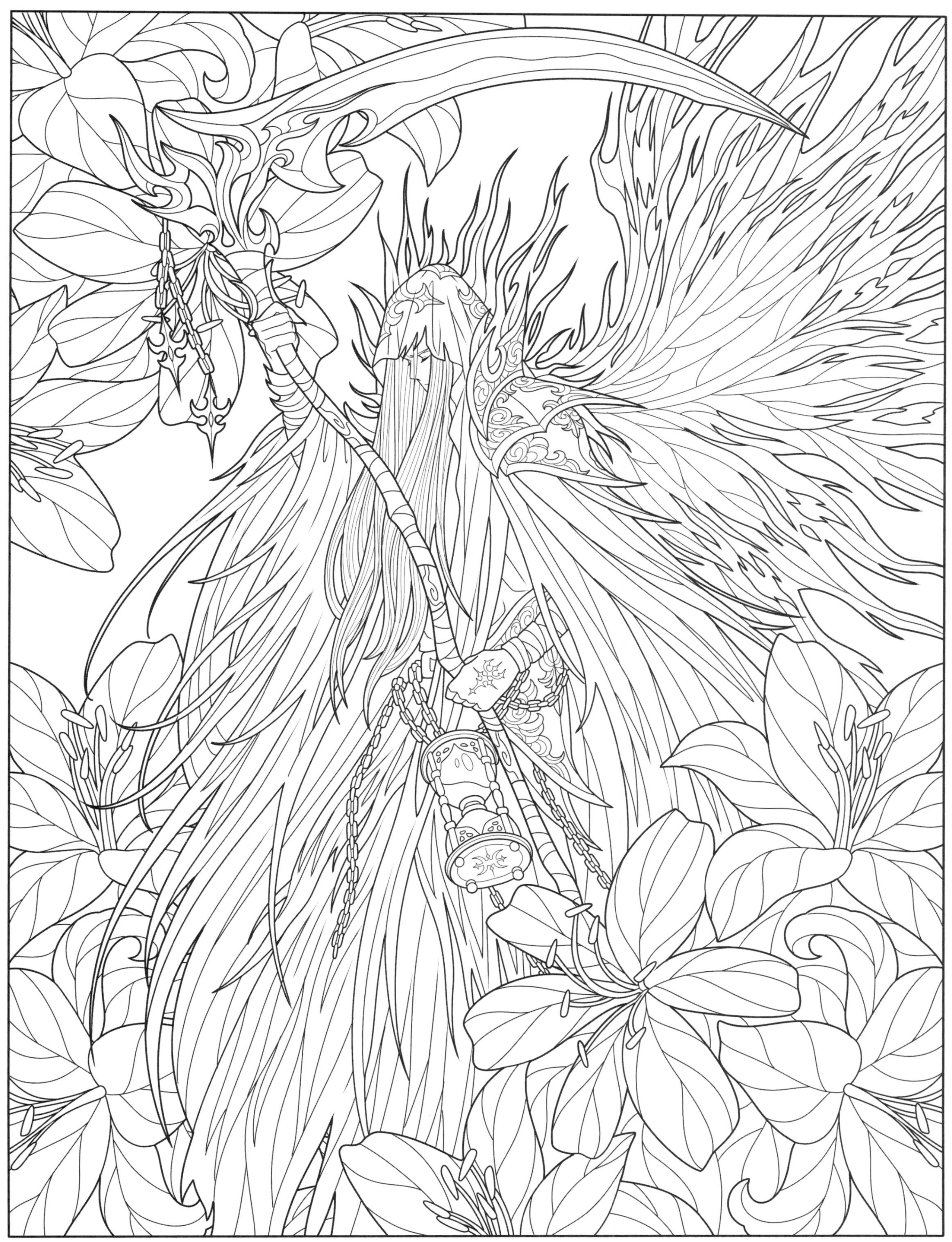

In the Murky Depths

Queen of creatures in deep, dark waters.

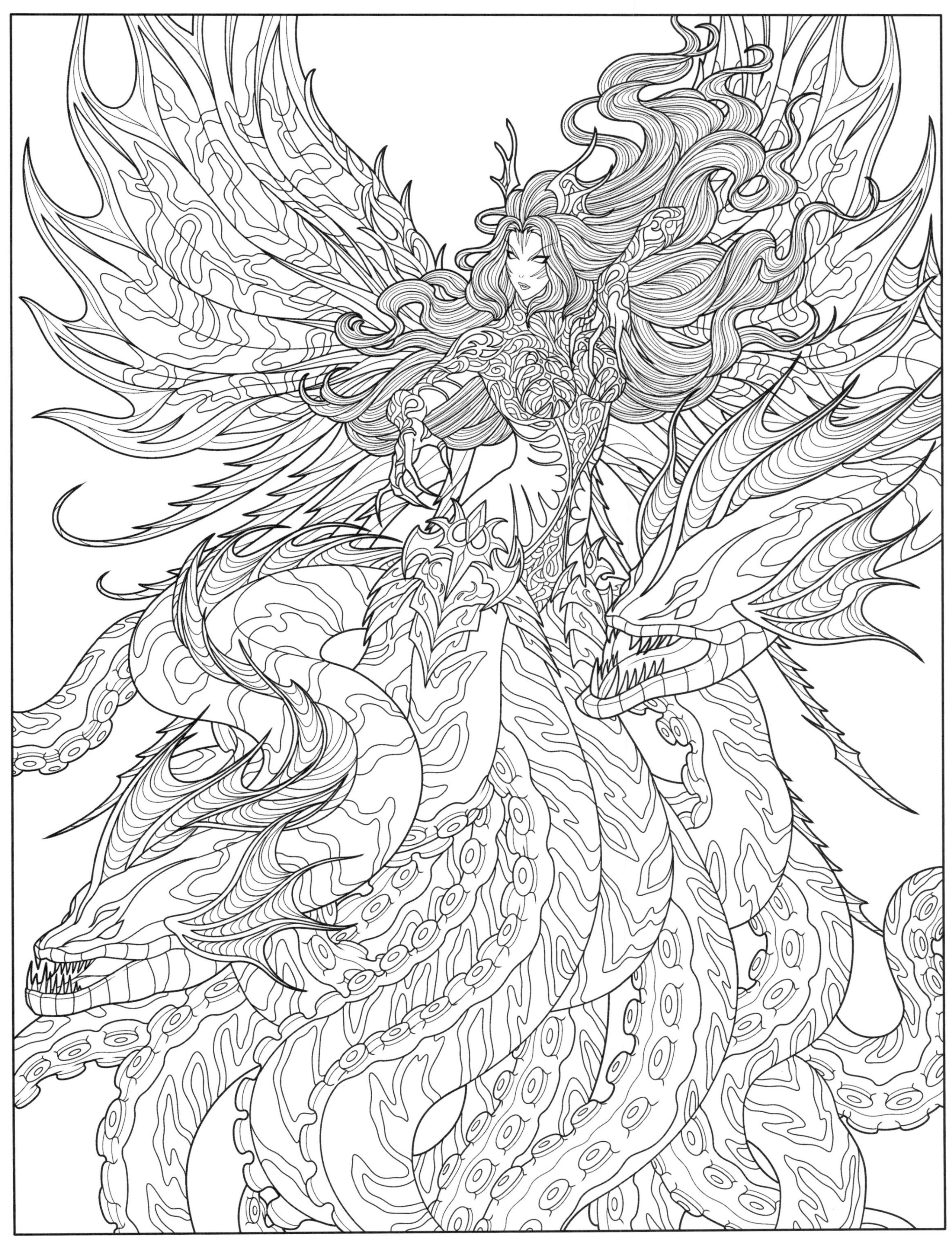

Flames of the Fire Fairy

Fiercely ablaze with a burning glow.

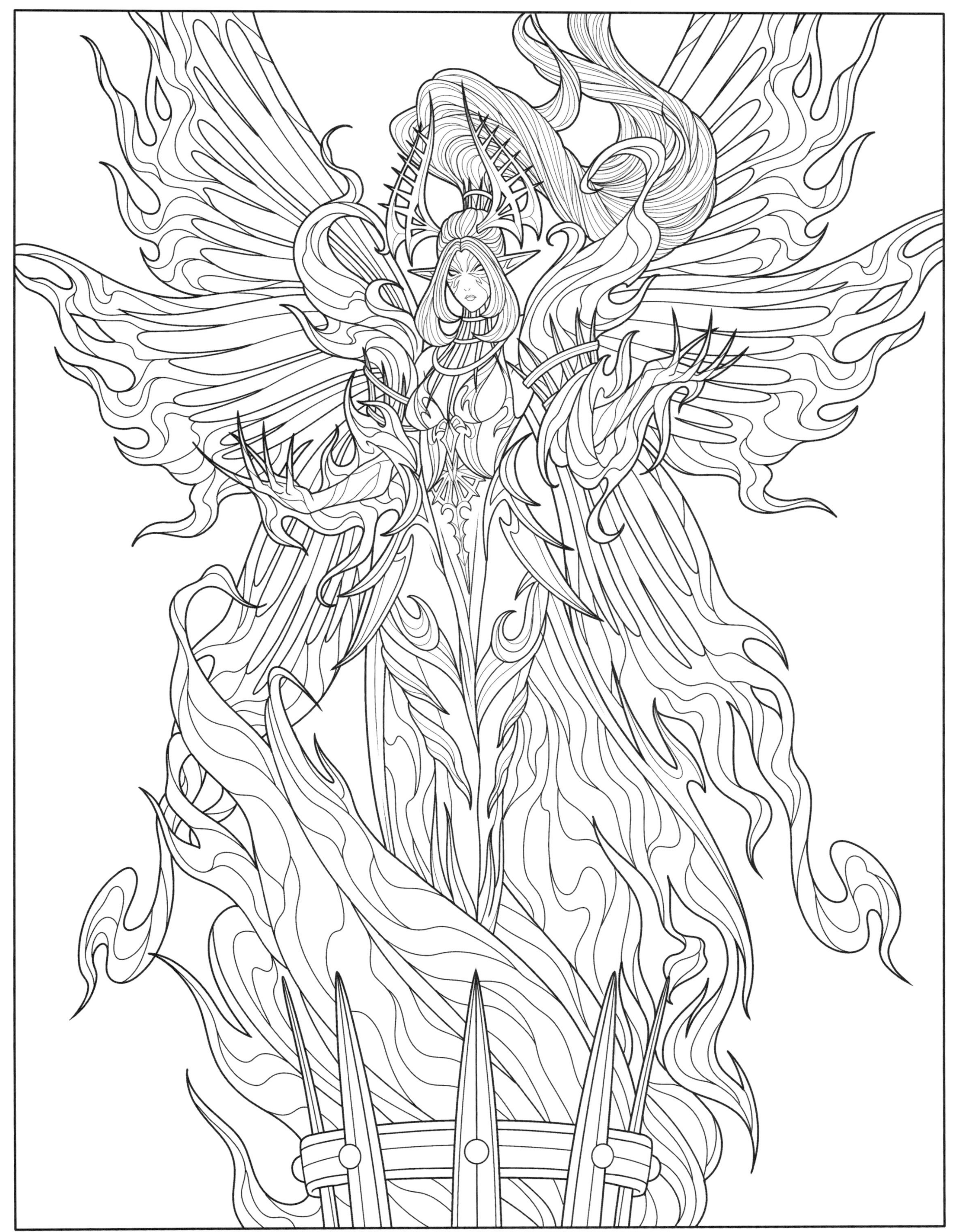

Crystal Magic

Harnessing the powerful energies of dark crystals.

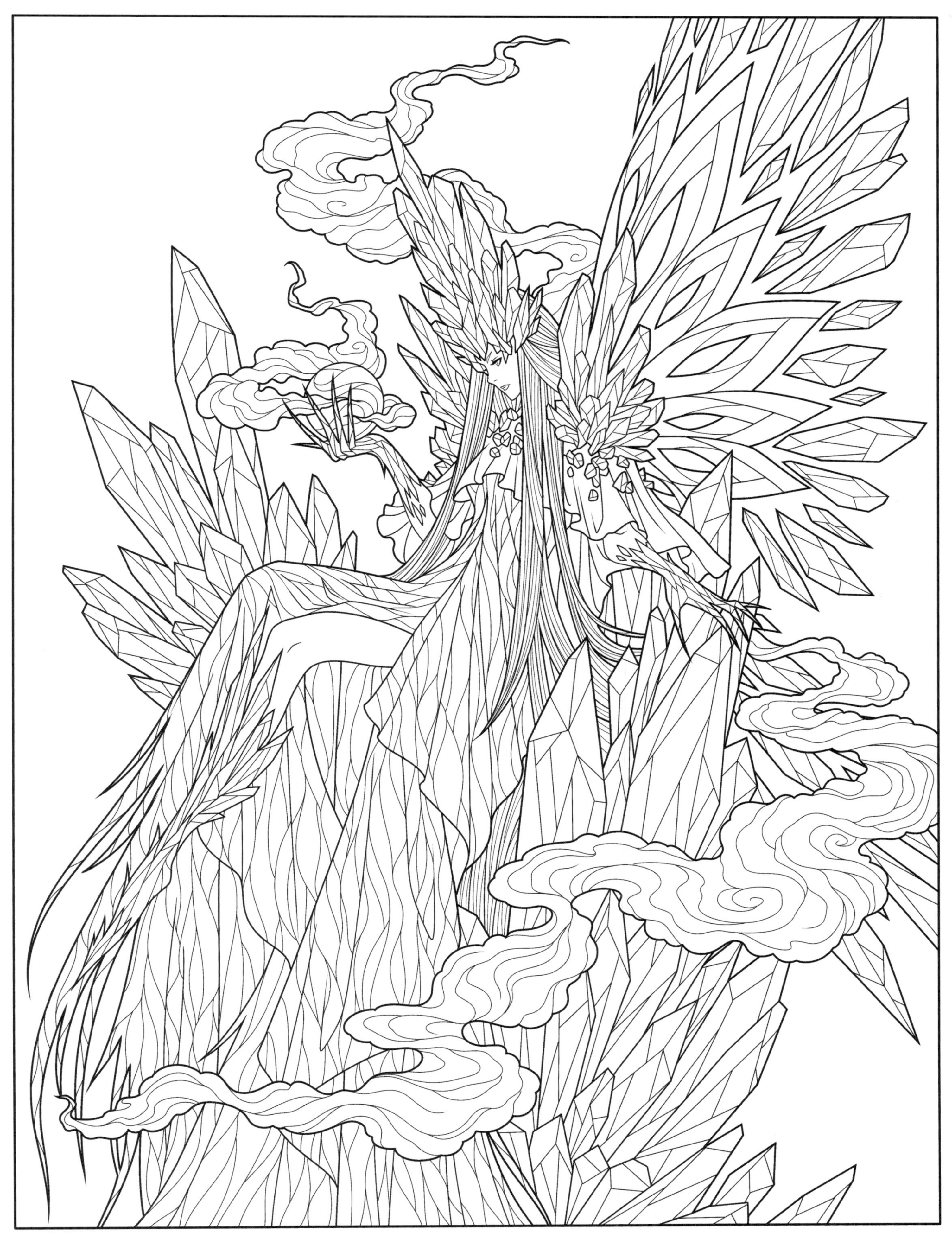

Spirit of the Underworld

Harbinger of death and destiny.

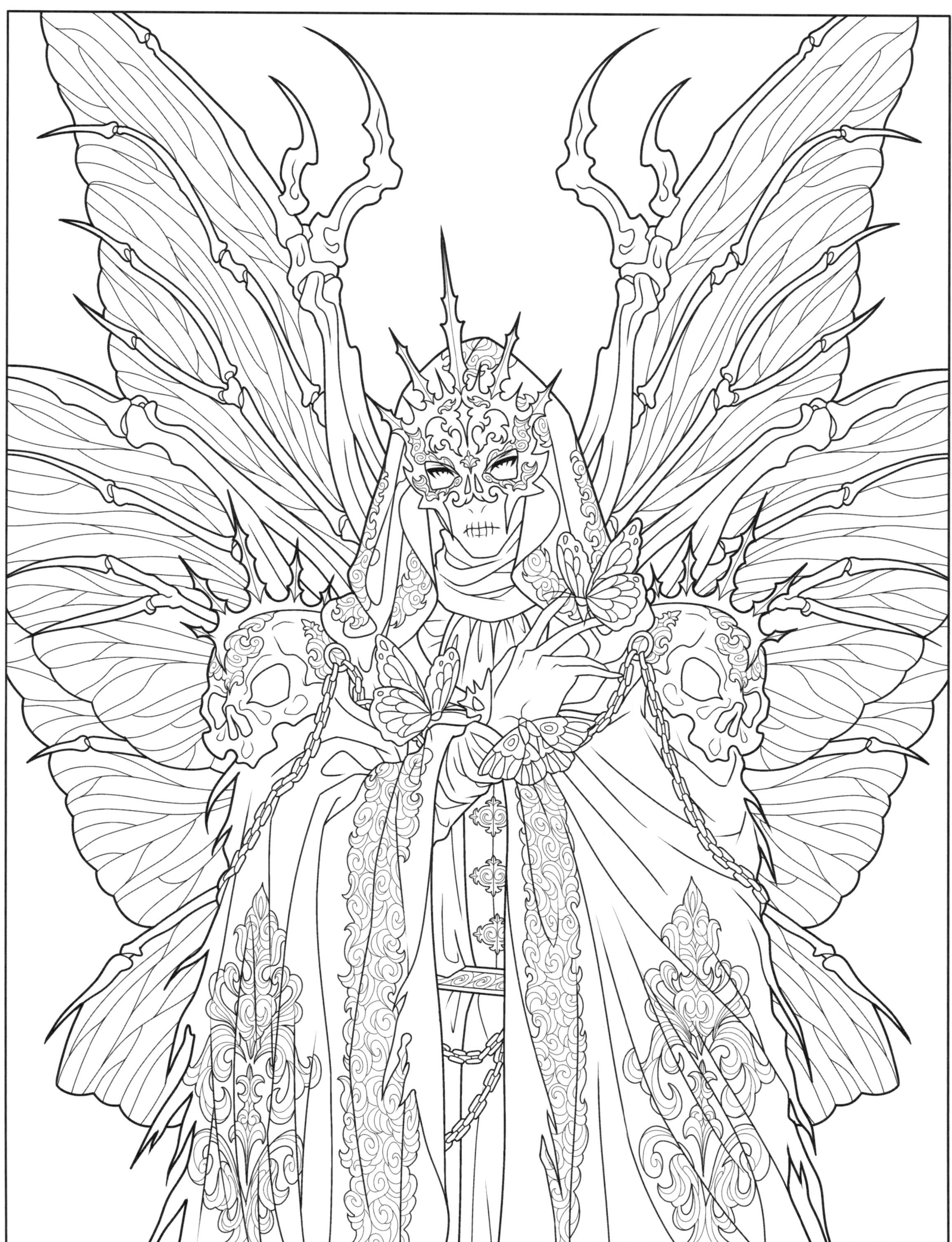

The Vampires' Embrace

Eternally united under a full moon.

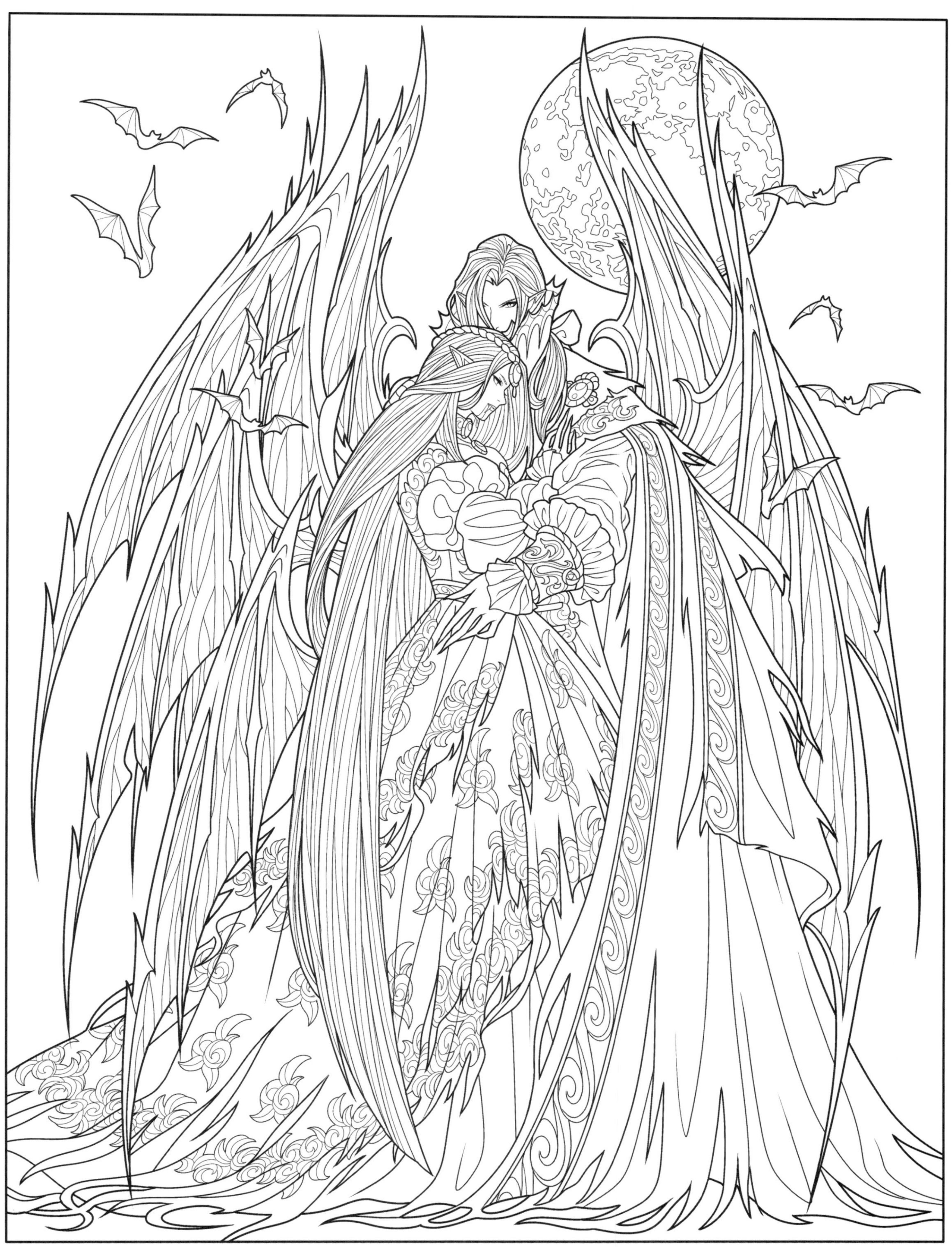

Among the Toadstools

Sitting atop poisonous fungi.

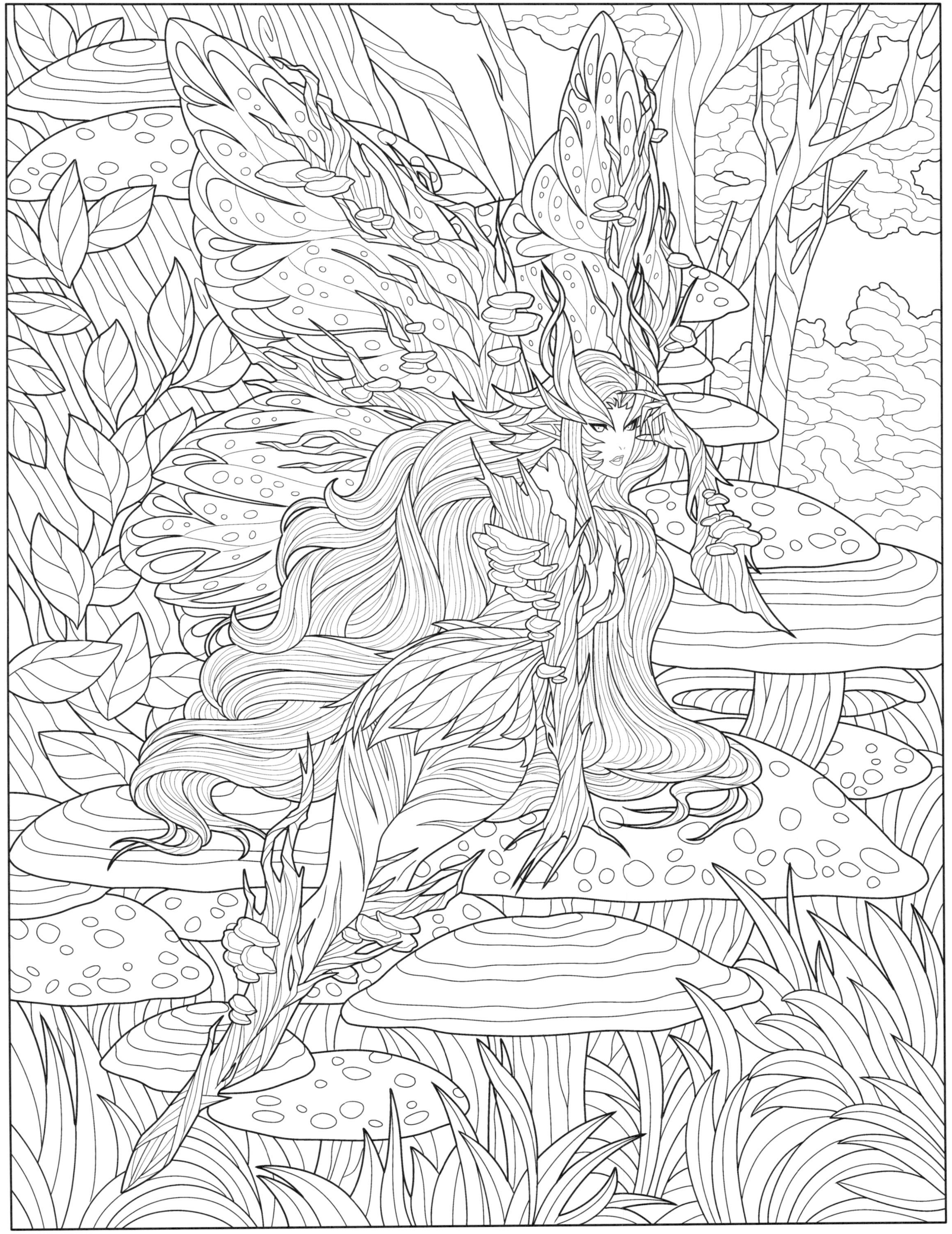

Dragon Princess

The powerful companion of a dangerous creature.

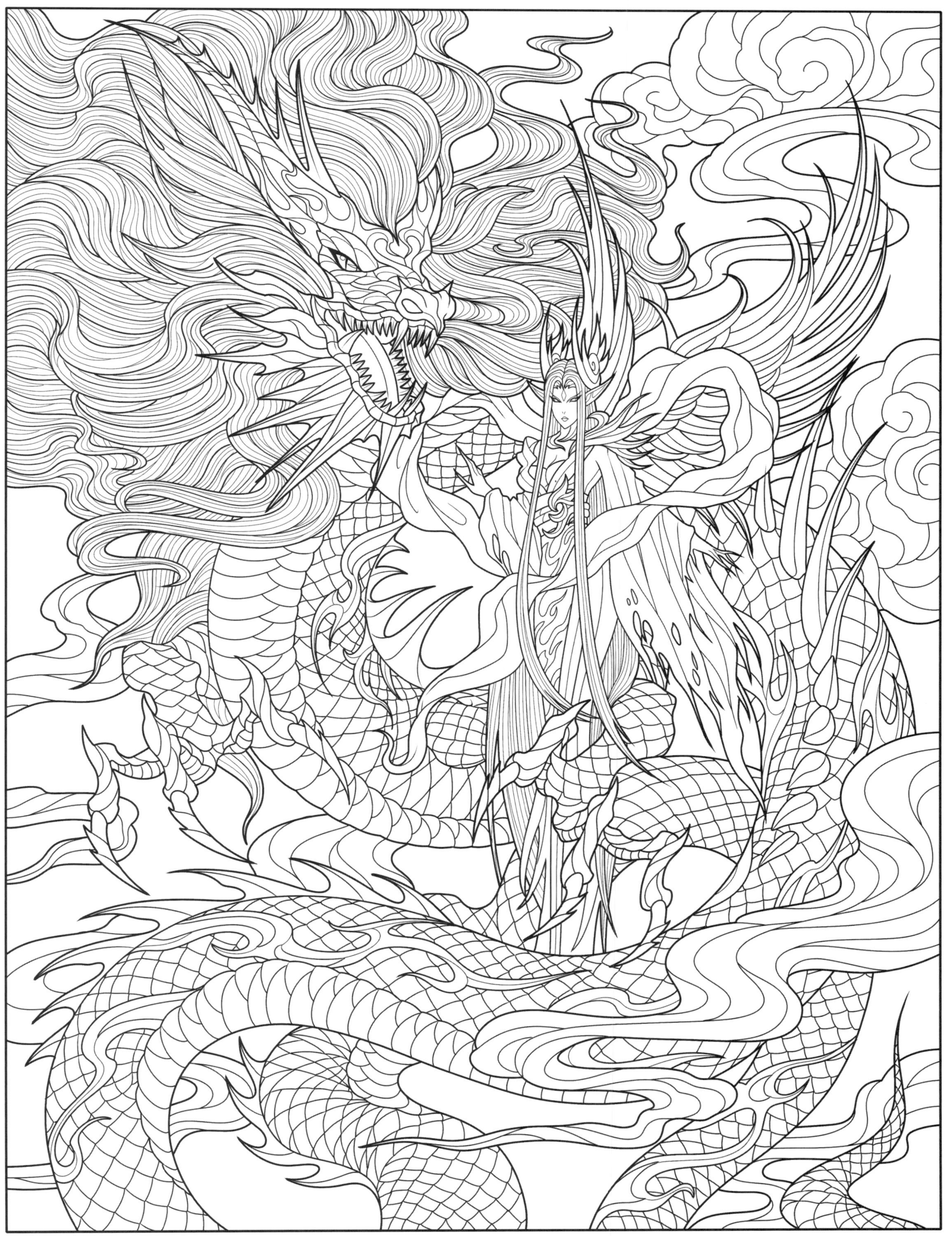

Kingdom of Goblins

Dweller of caves and bringer of mischief.

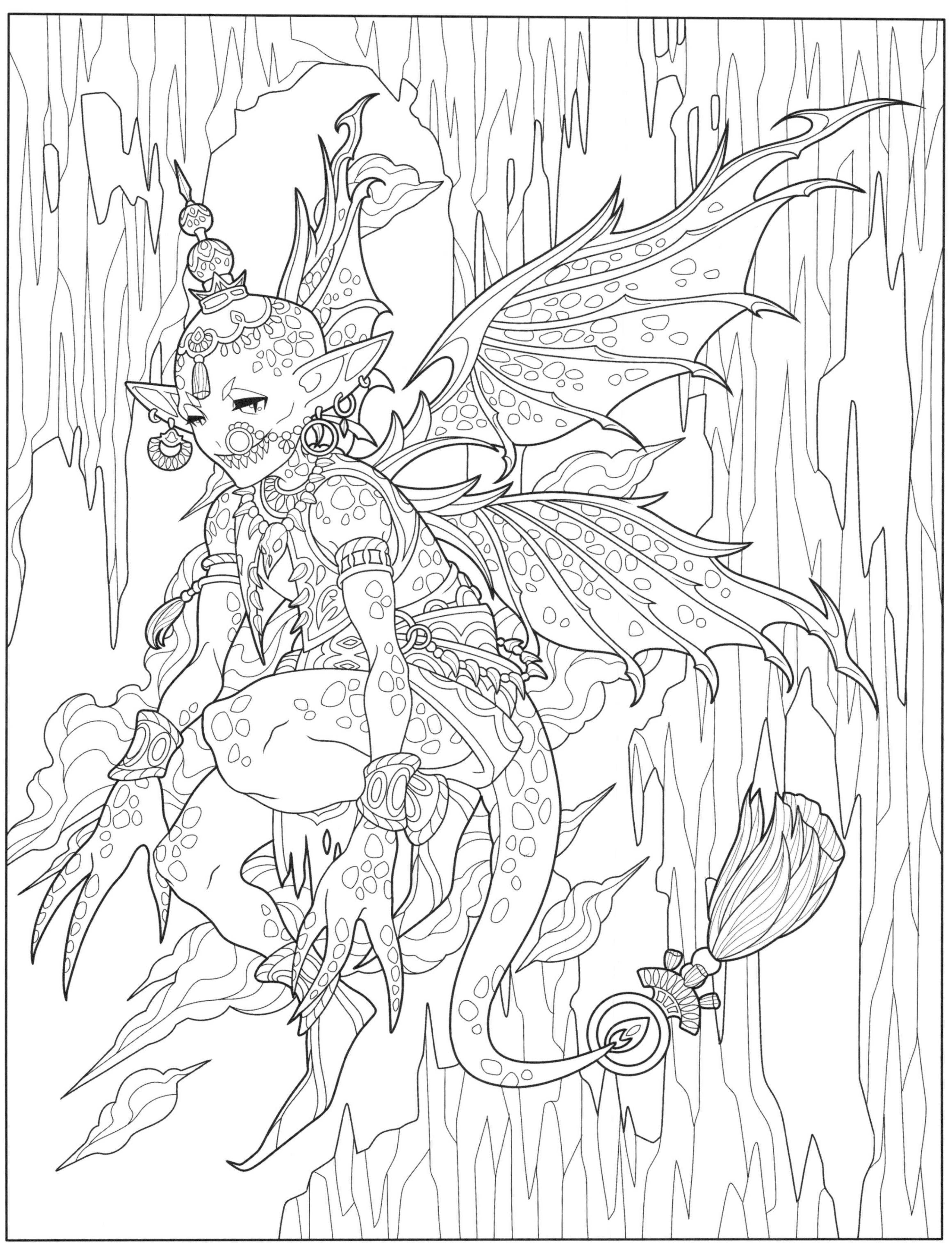

The Ways of the Raven

Flying into eternal darkness.

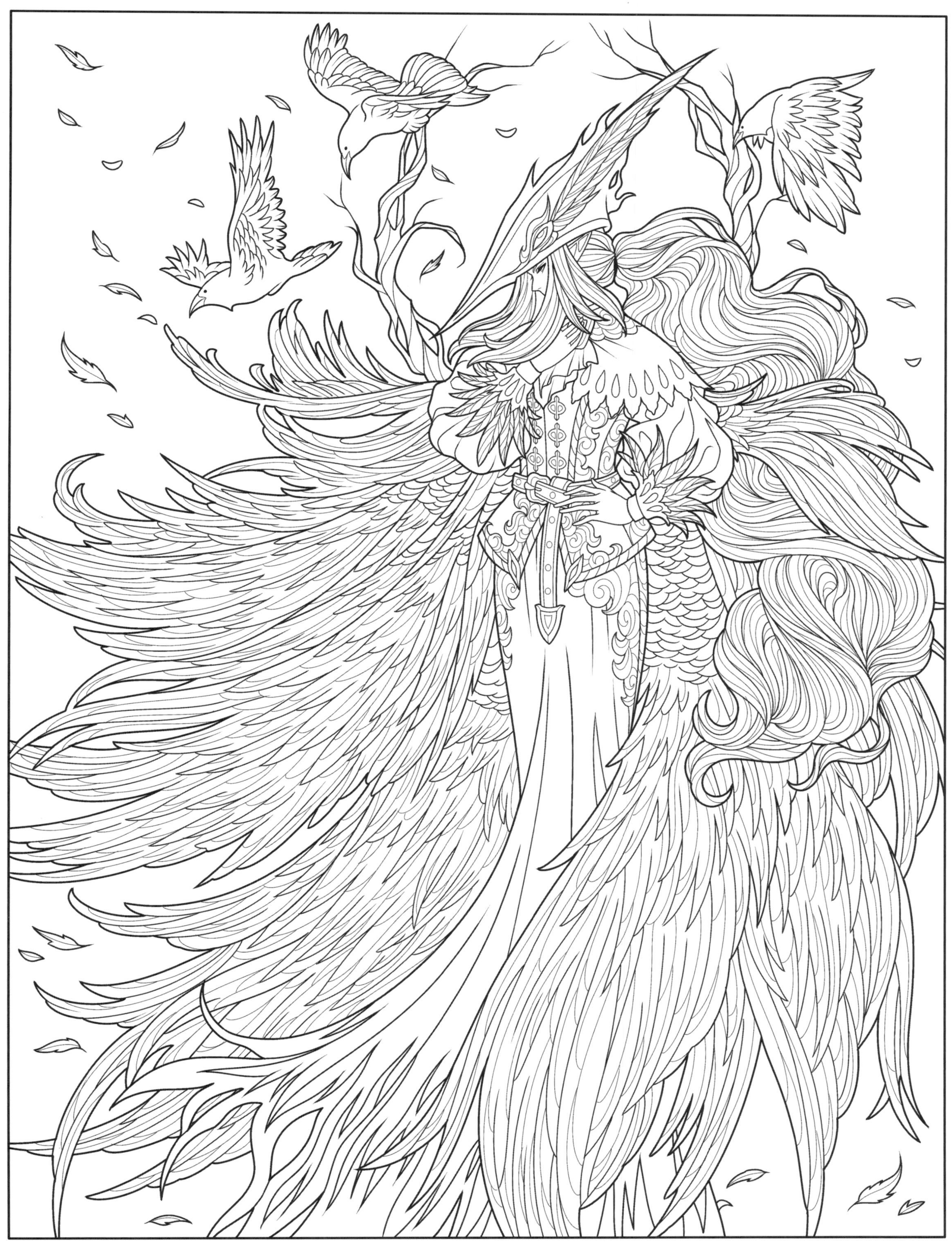

The Clown's Playroom

A terrifying show of trickery and deception.

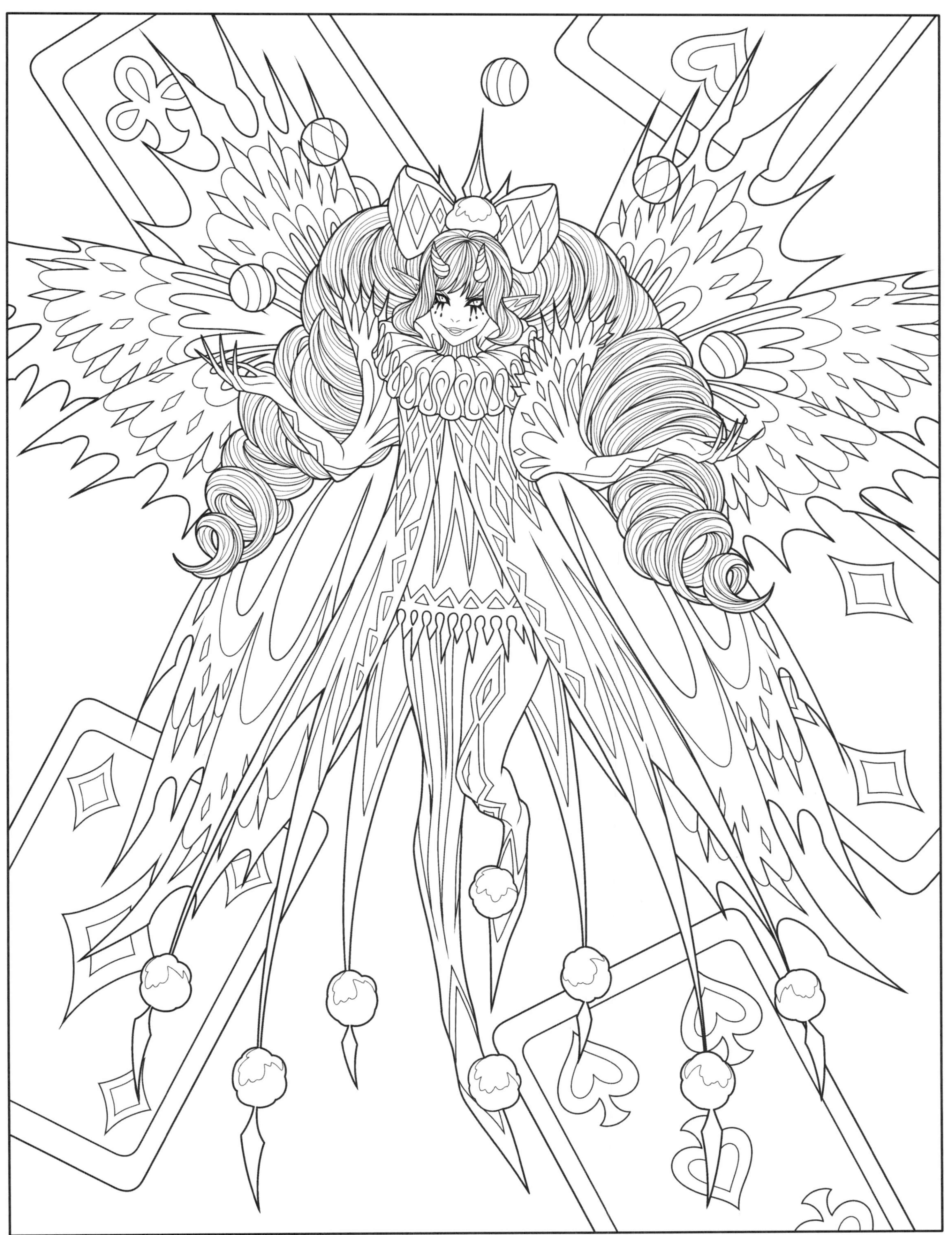

Fairy of the Thorn

A flower of evil in full bloom.

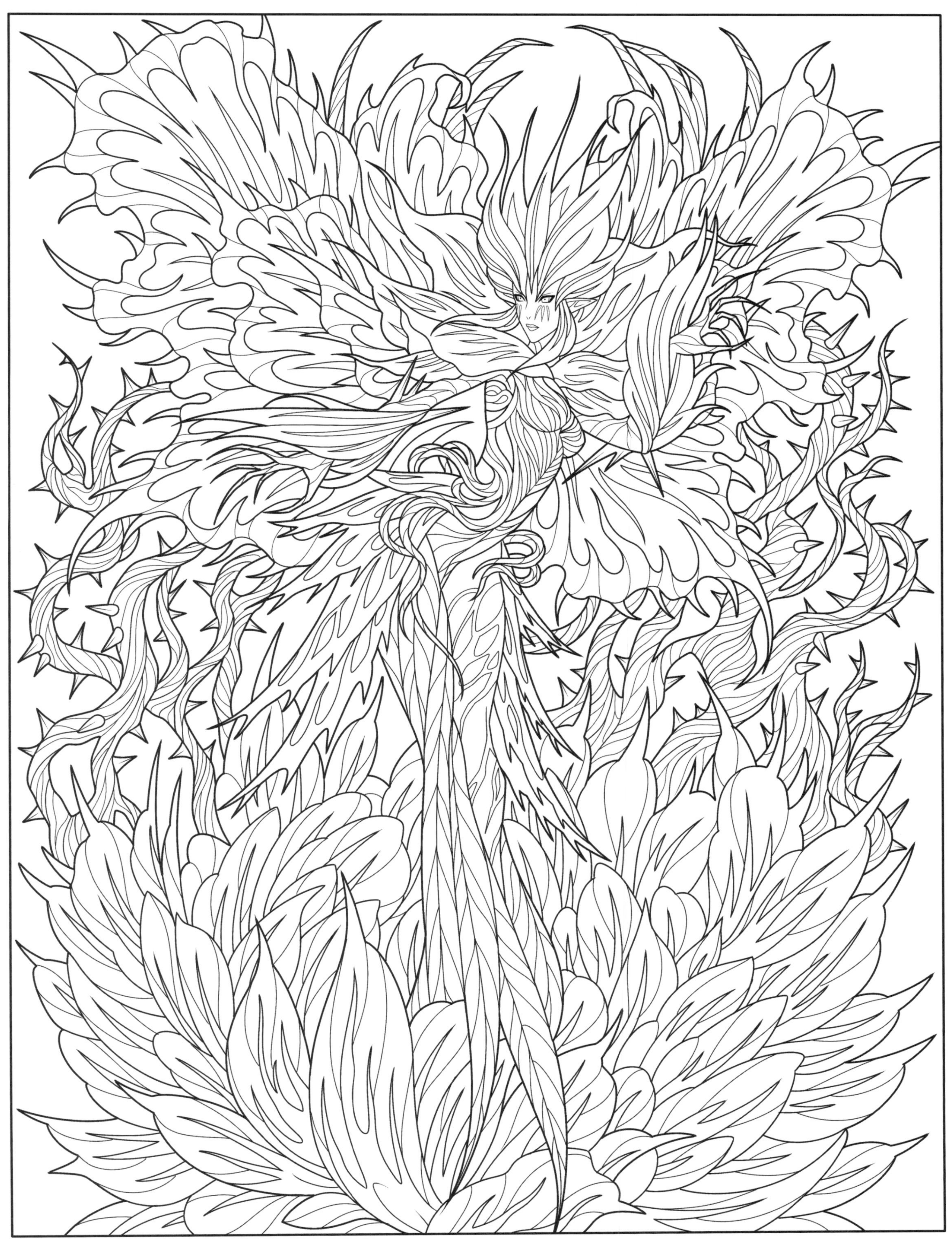

Lord of the Stags

Ruler of creatures in dark, enchanted forests.

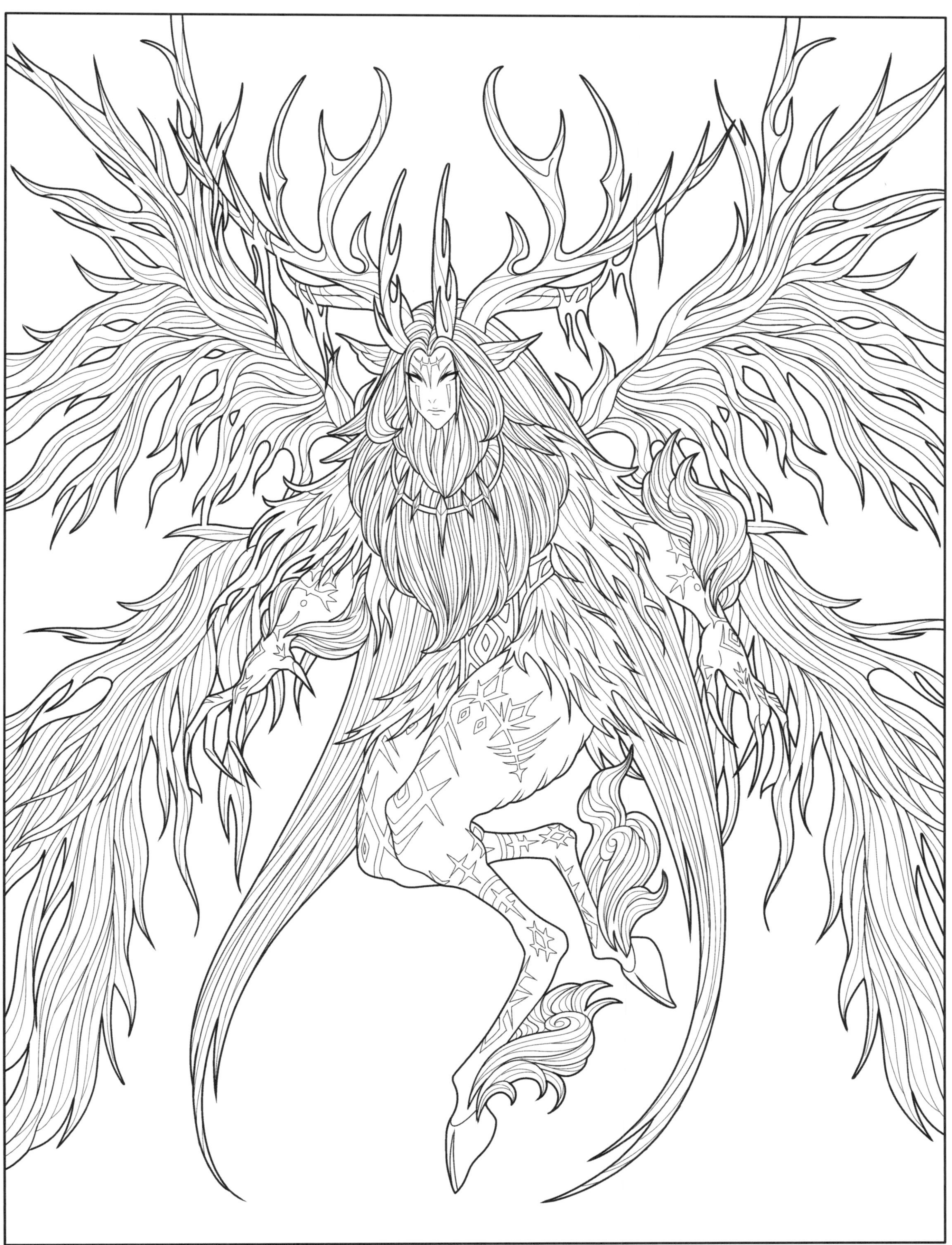

A Chilling Touch

Queen of the ice fairies with coldness in her heart.

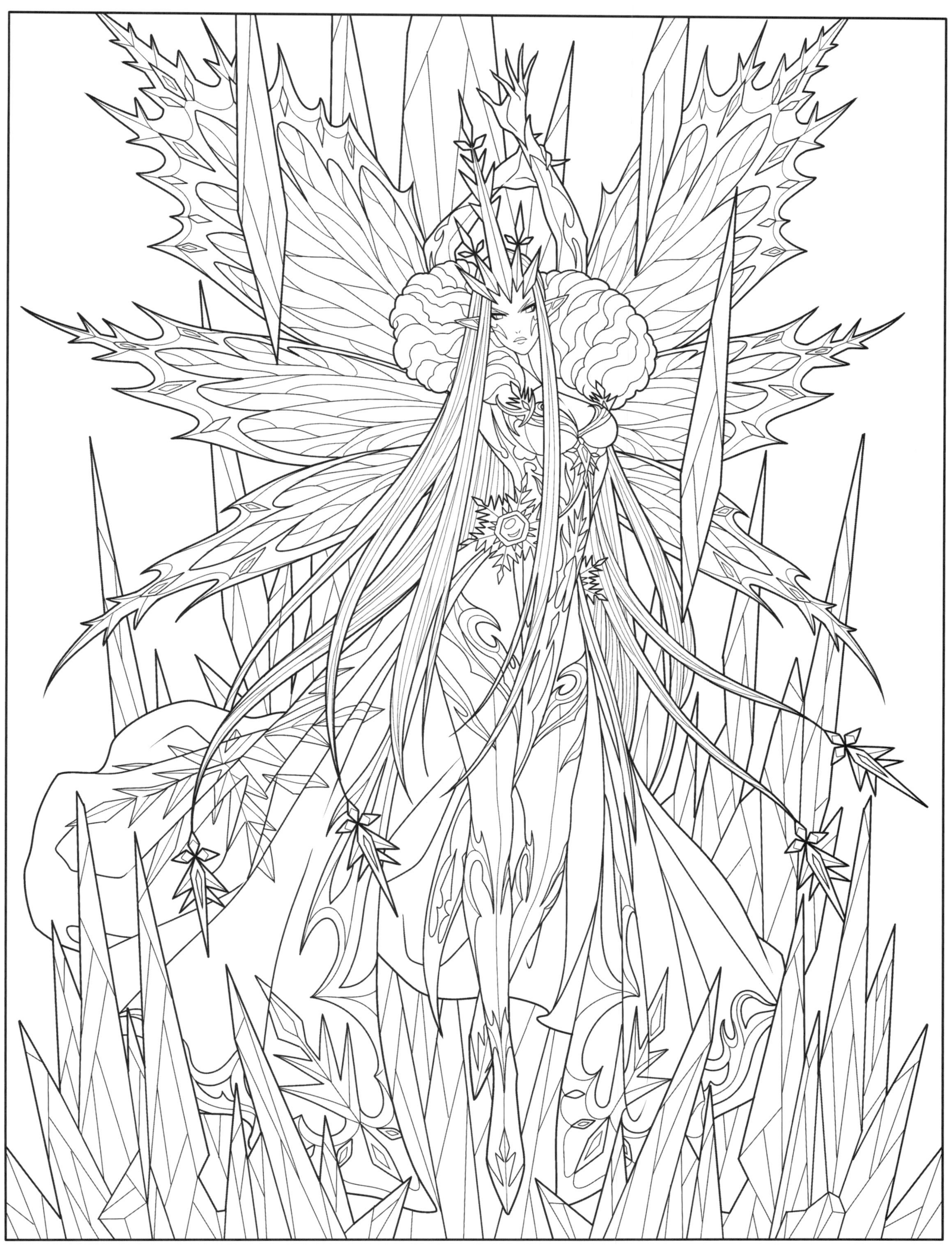

Mystical Moths

Concealed in the darkness of night.

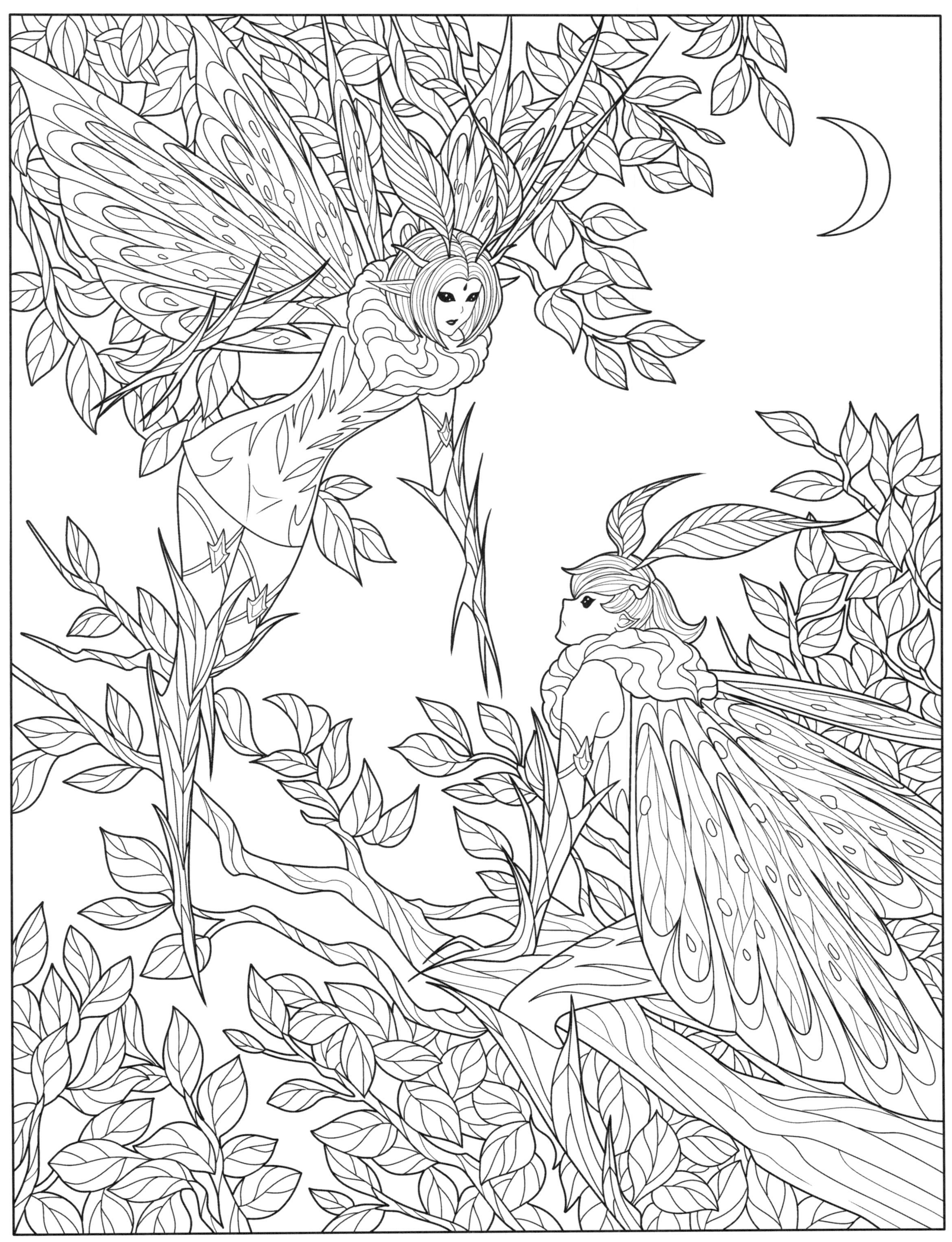

Psychic Power

Divining dark futures from her crystal ball.

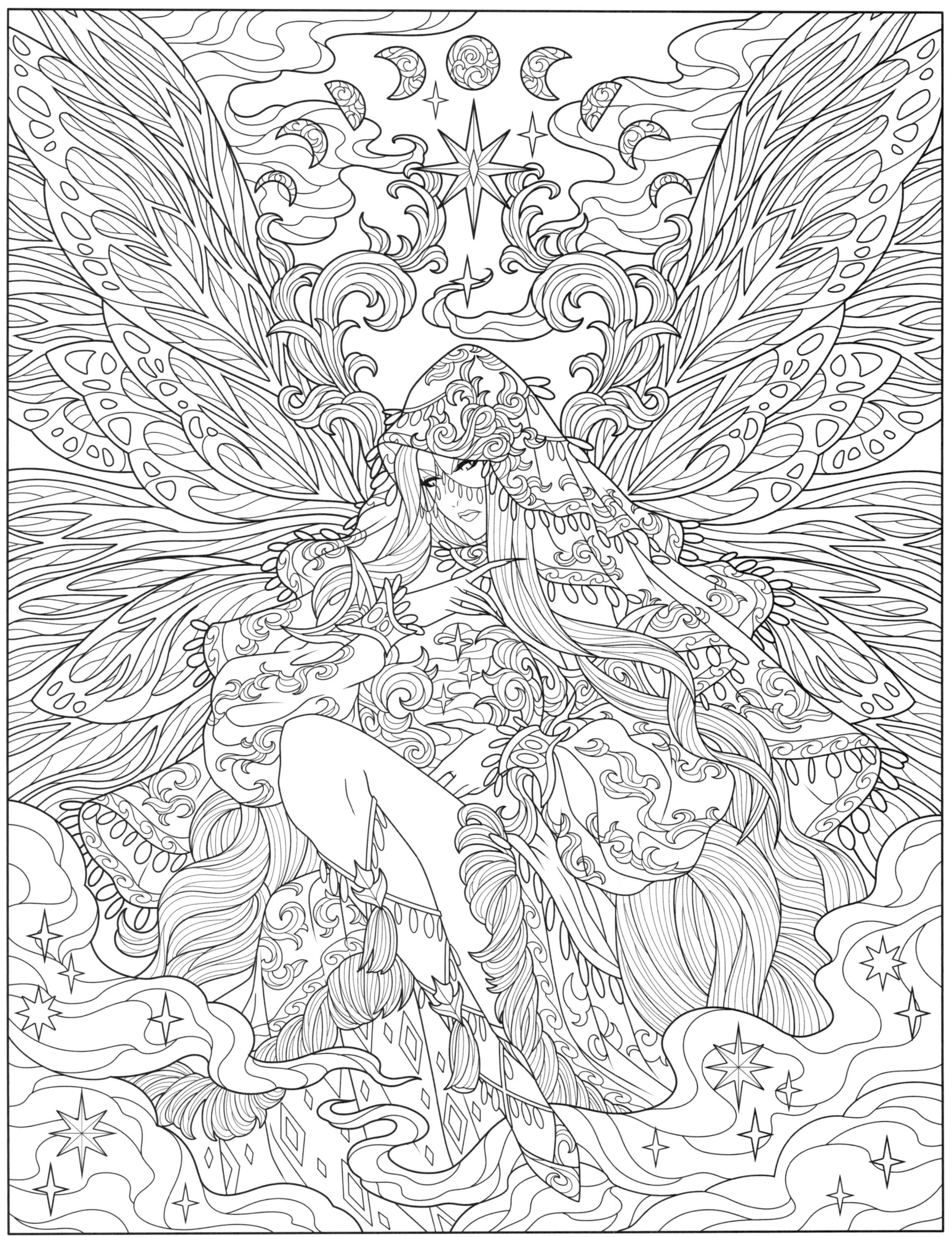

Legend of the Werewolf

Servant of the moon with supernatural strength.

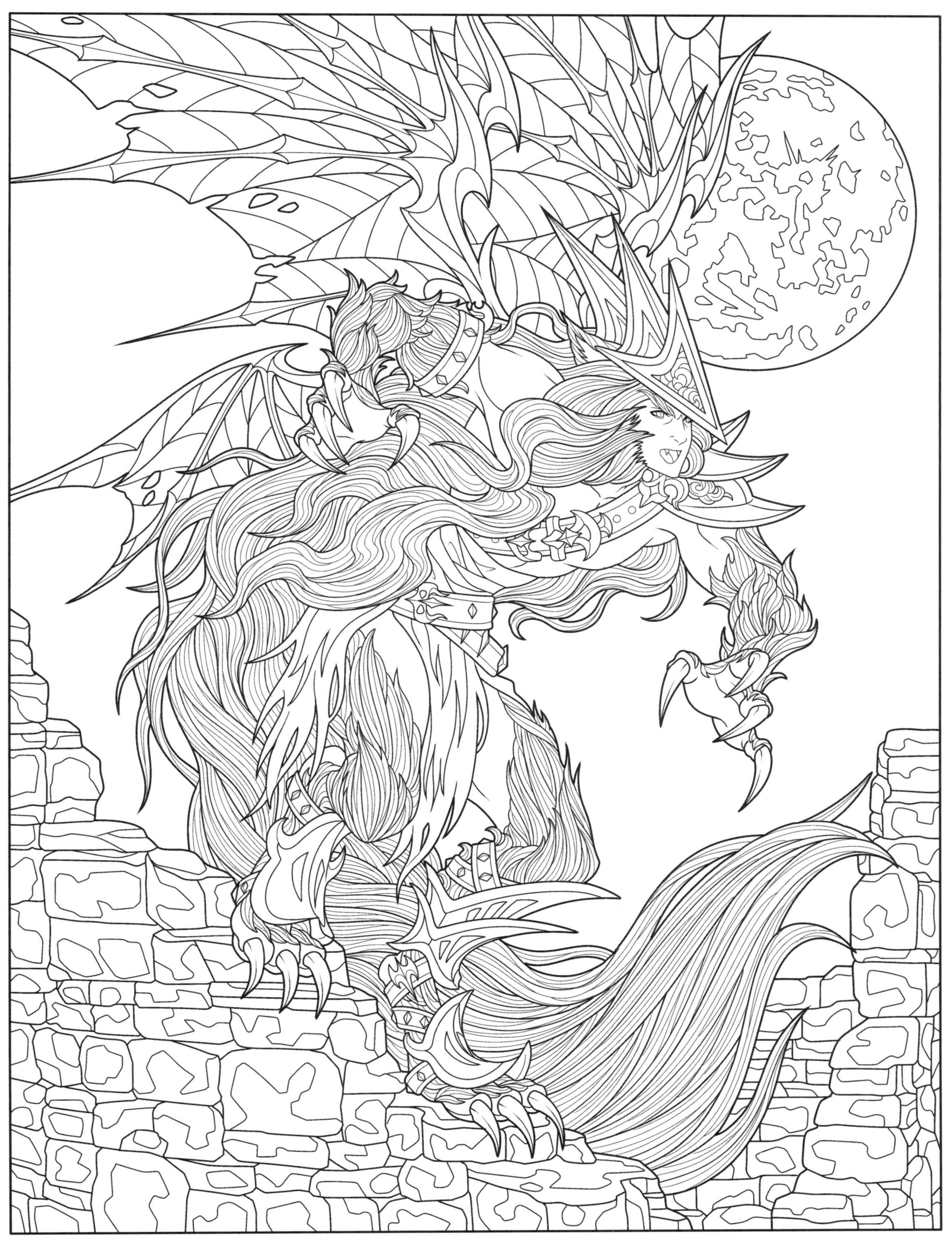

Serpentine Queen

Empress of snakes with a venomous gaze.

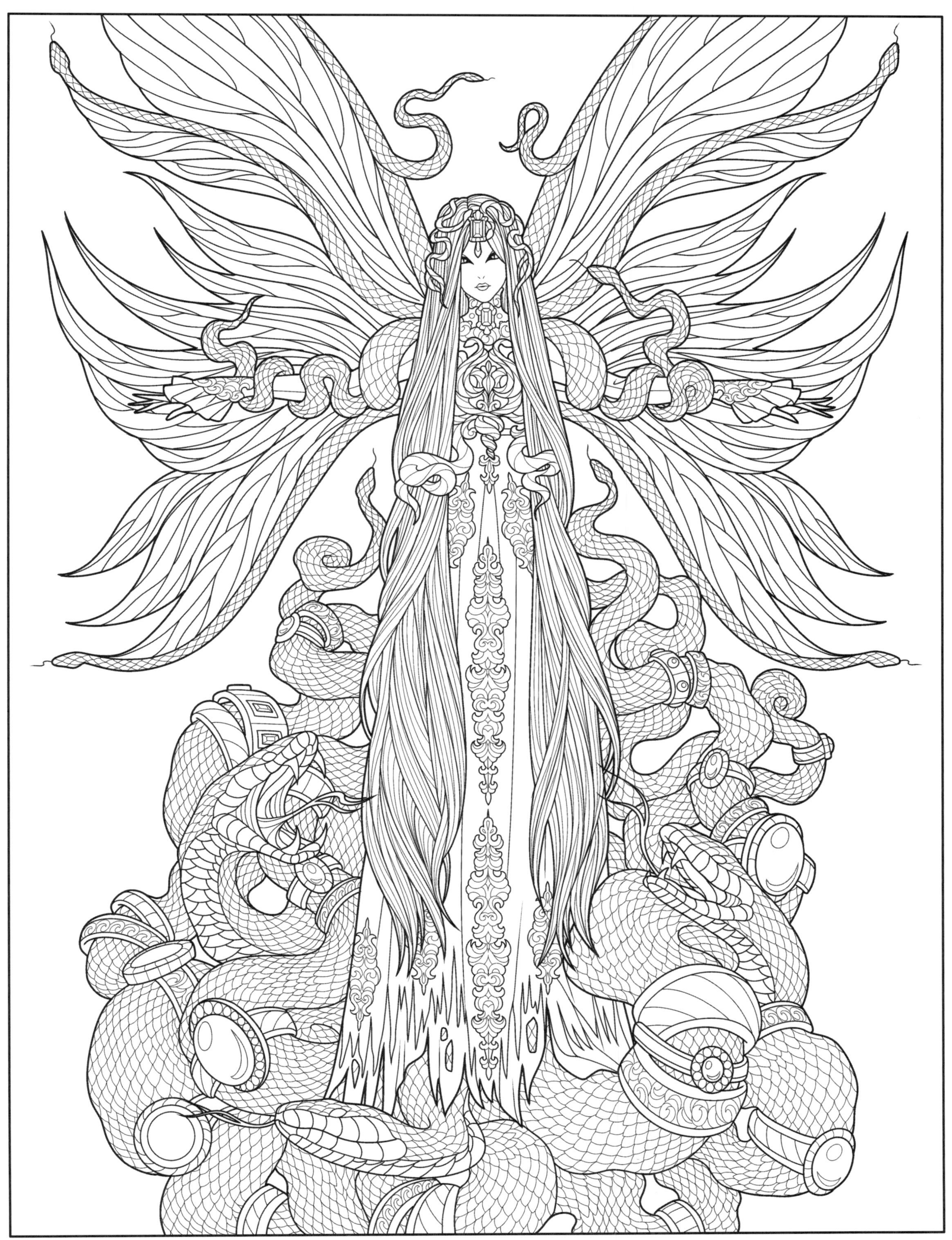

Song of the Siren

Alluring and haunting in the watery depths.

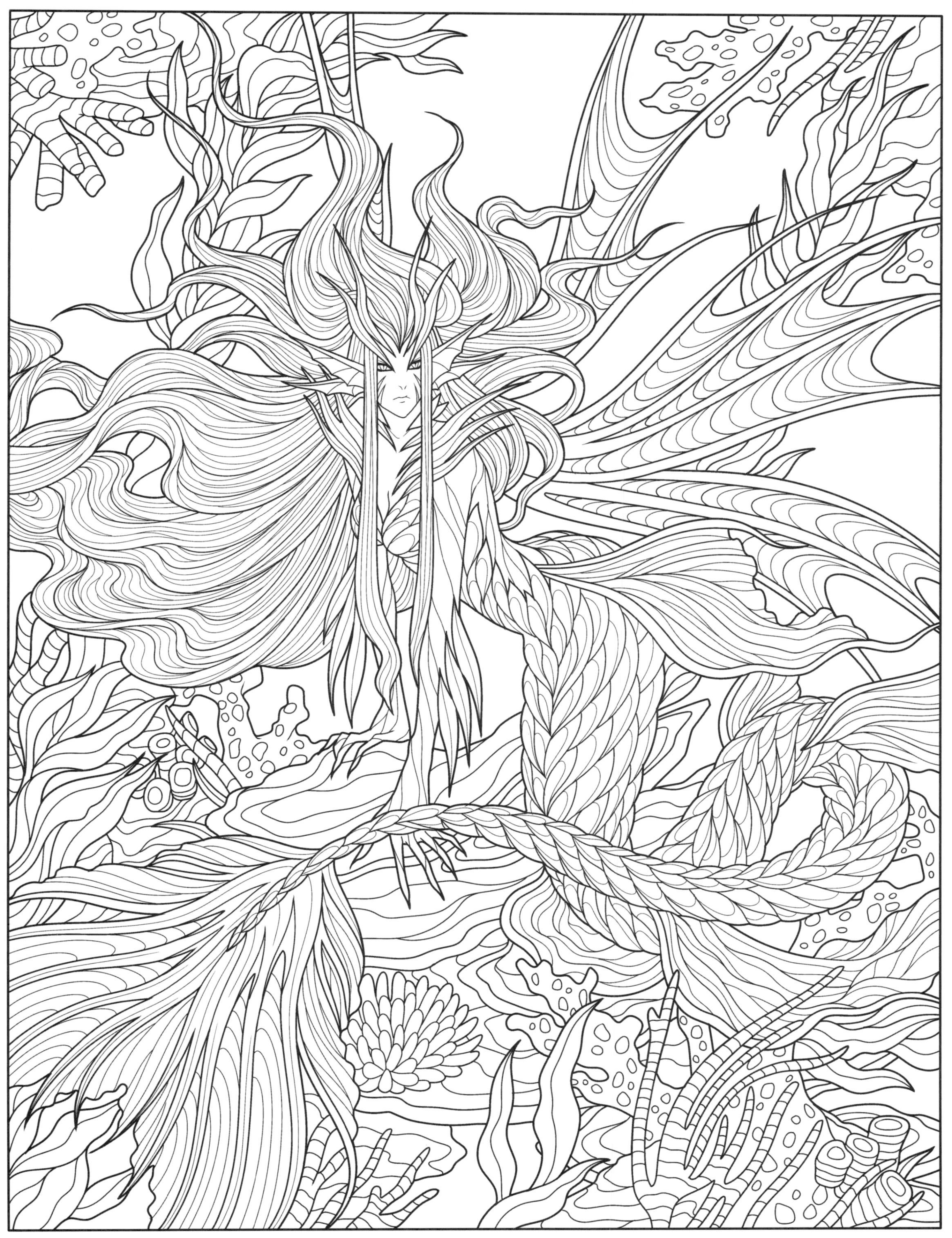

Creature of the Night

Emerging from the shadows after twilight.

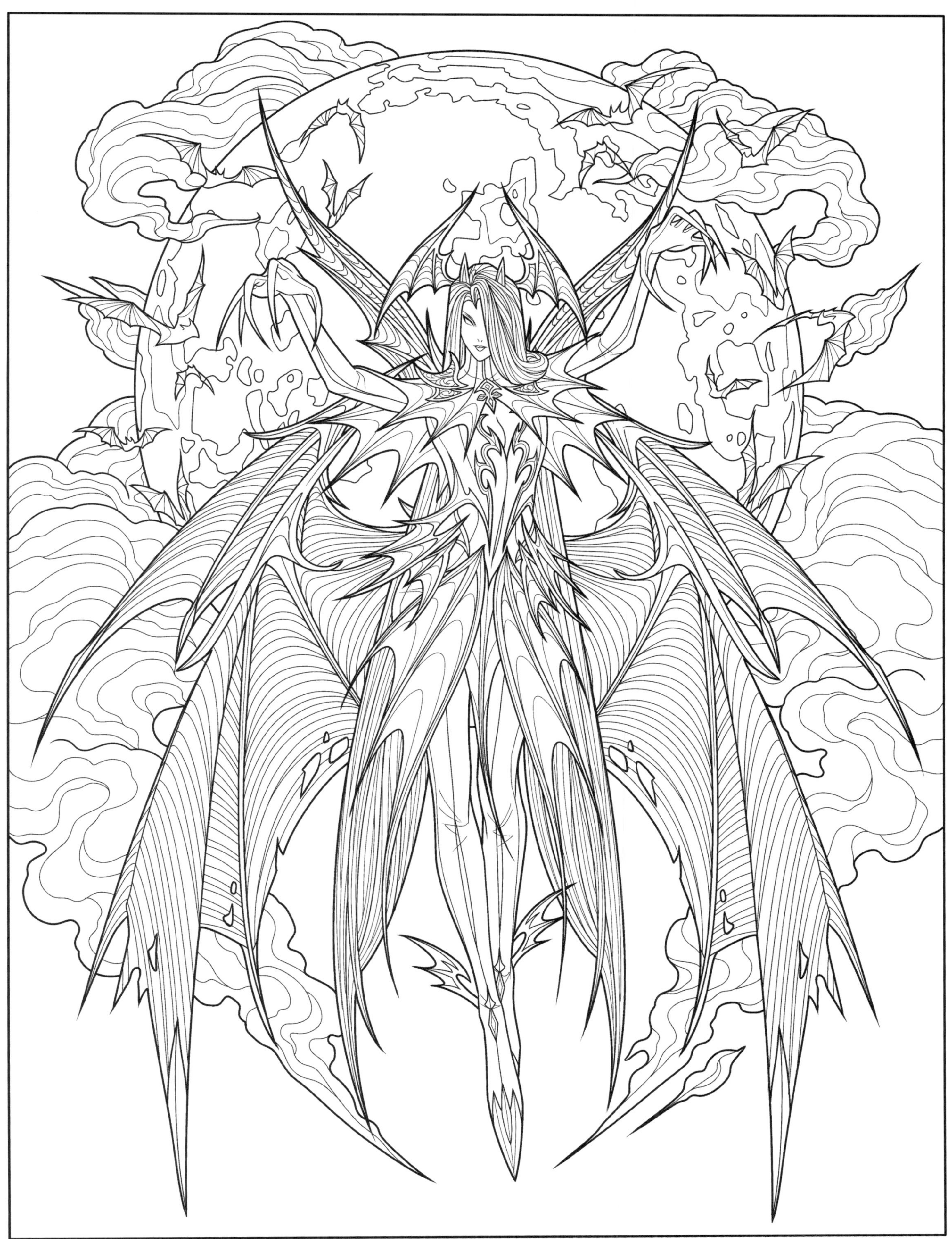

Clockwork Wings

A curious creature from a future world.

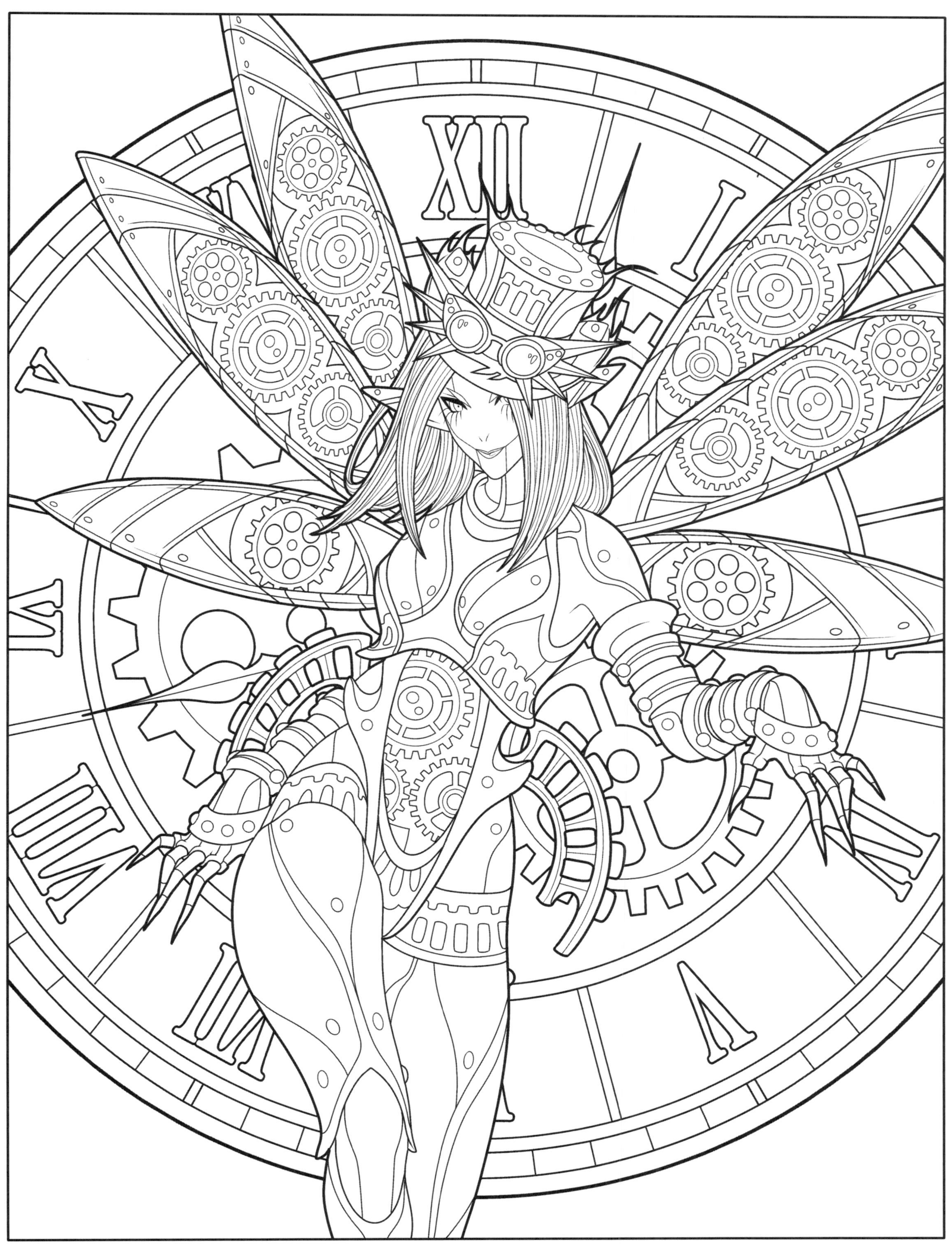

Rise of the Beetles

Indestructible armour and a true sense of spirit.

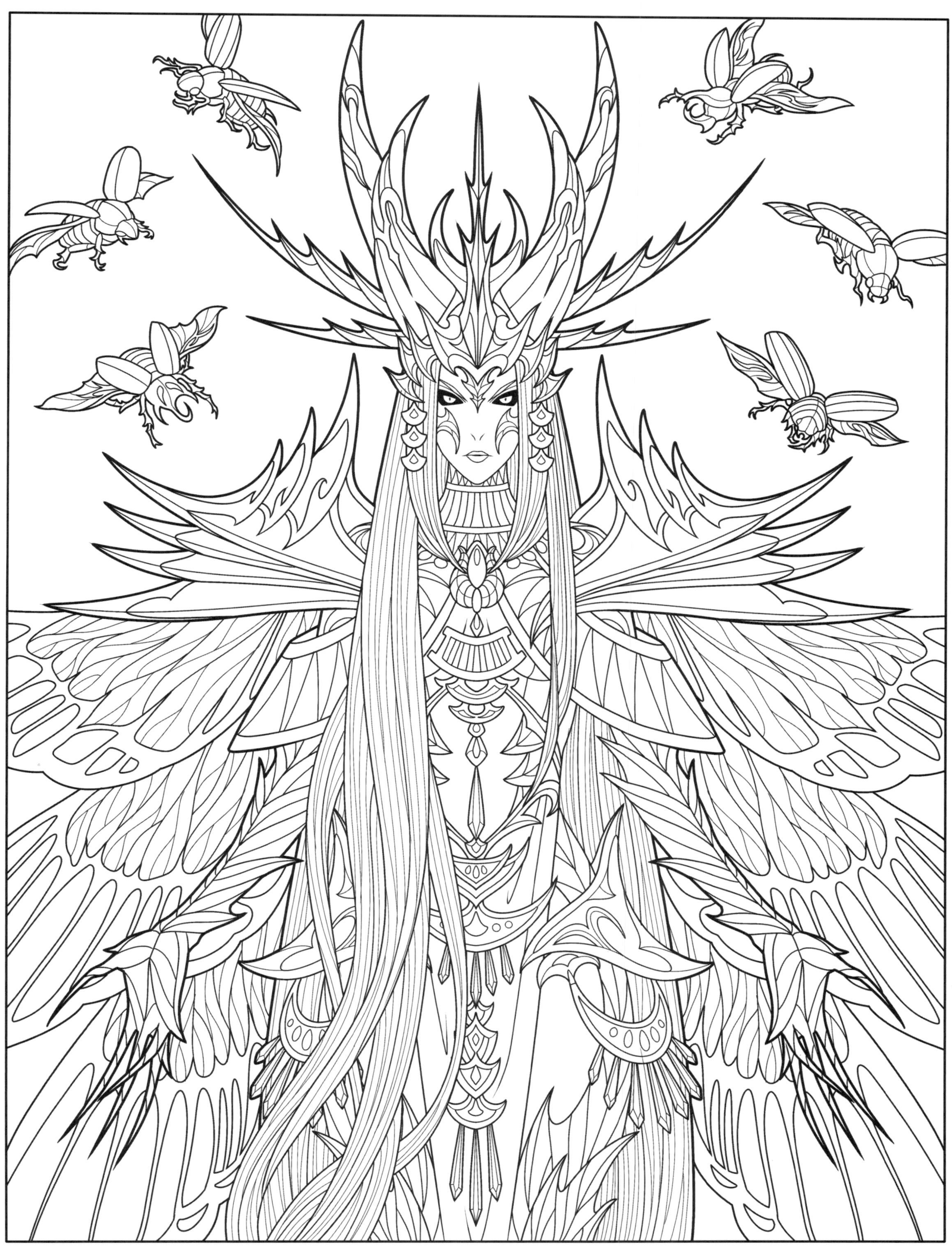

The Scorpion's Sting

Feared above all in vast deserts.

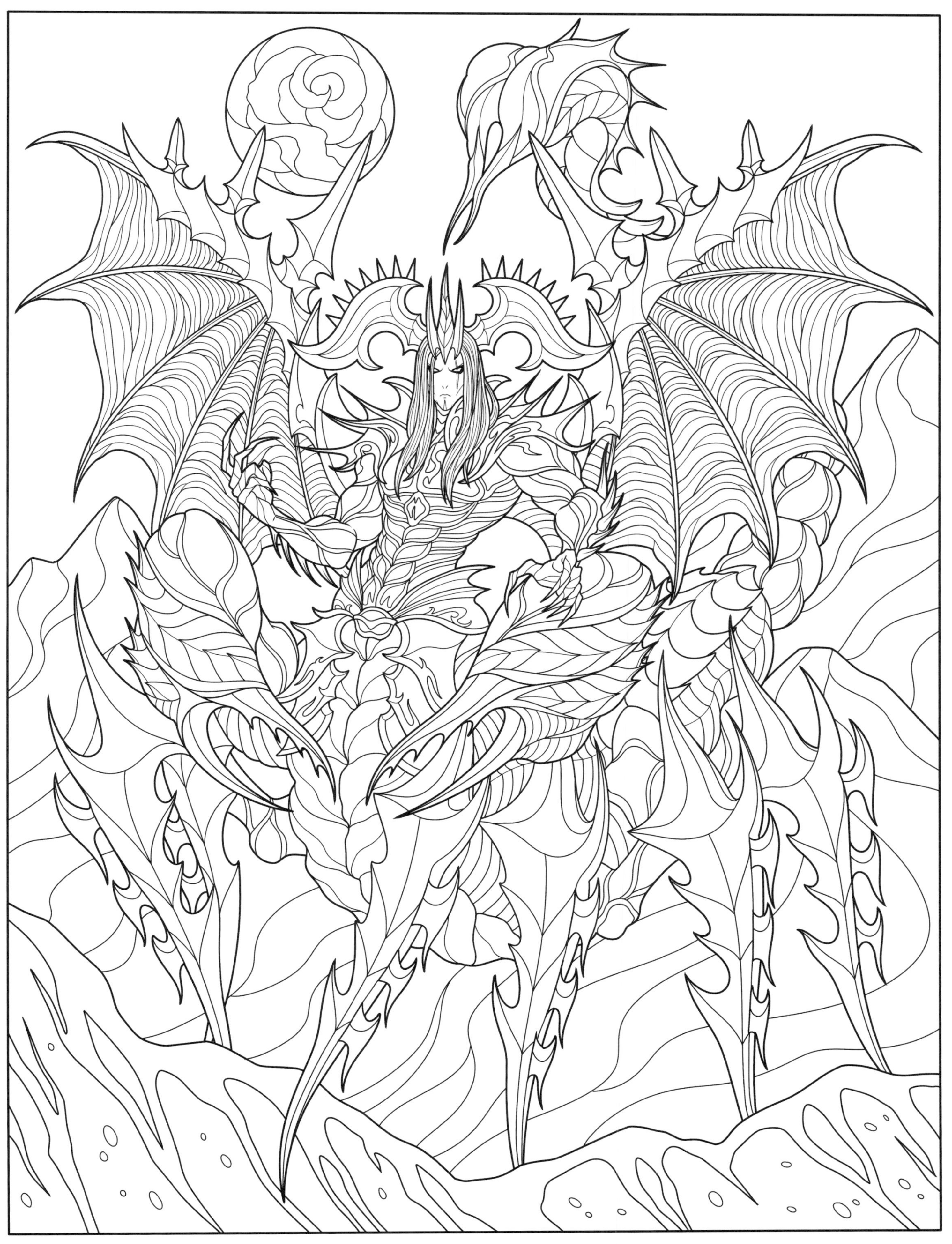

The Gothic Rose

The sharp thorn of a delicate flower.

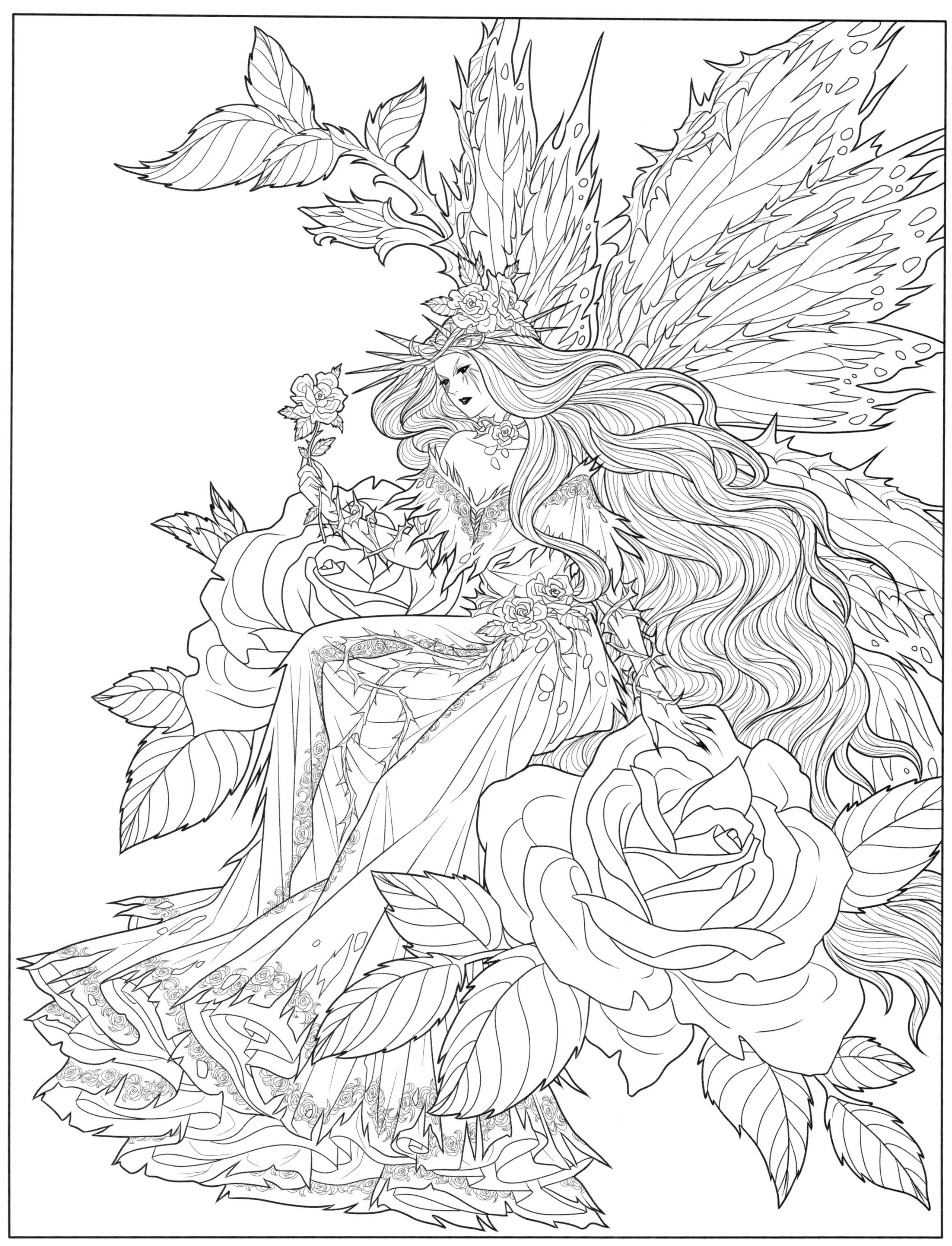

The Haunted Doll

A porcelain princess possessed by a sinister spirit.

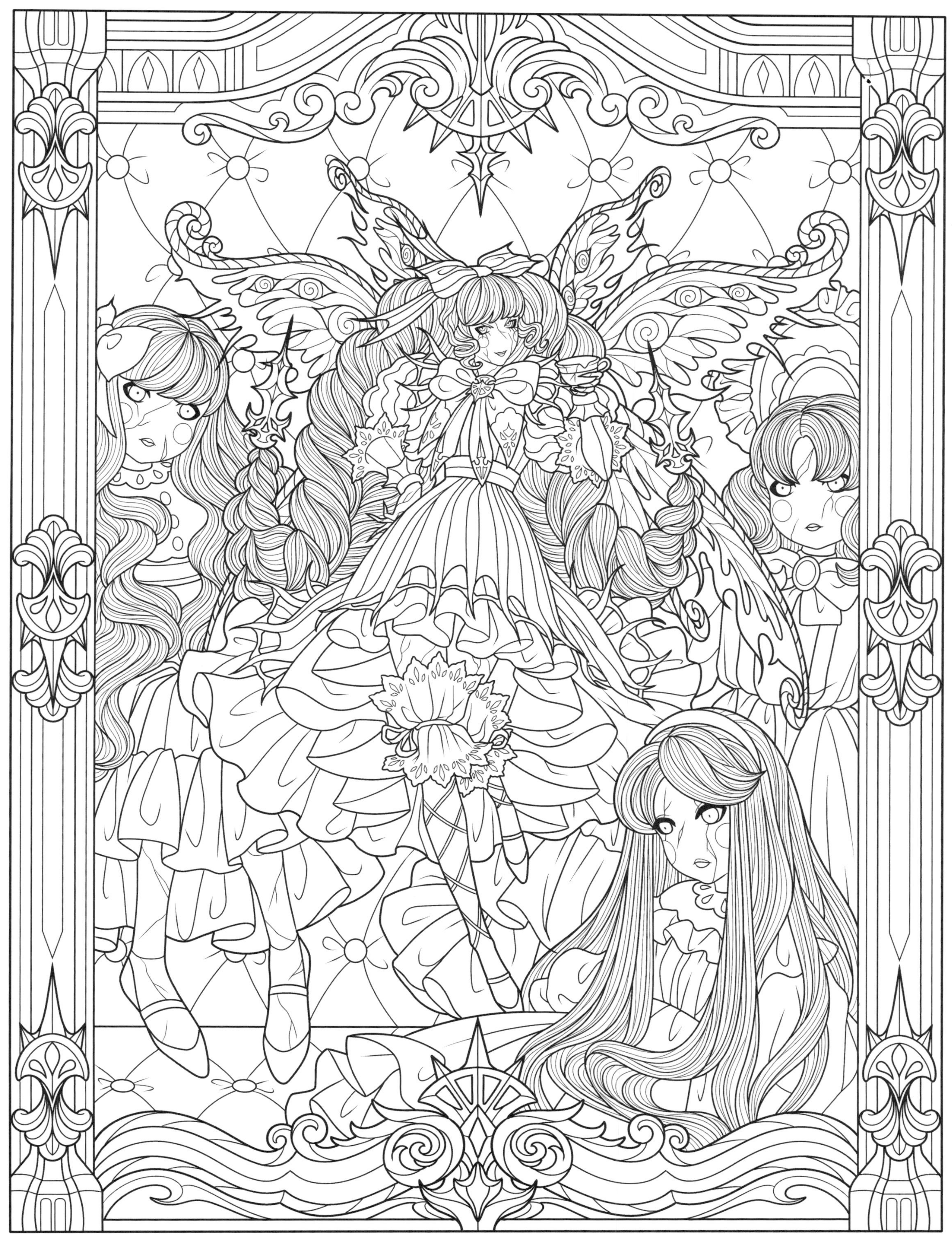

The Dragon Lord

Born of fire and ally of dragons.

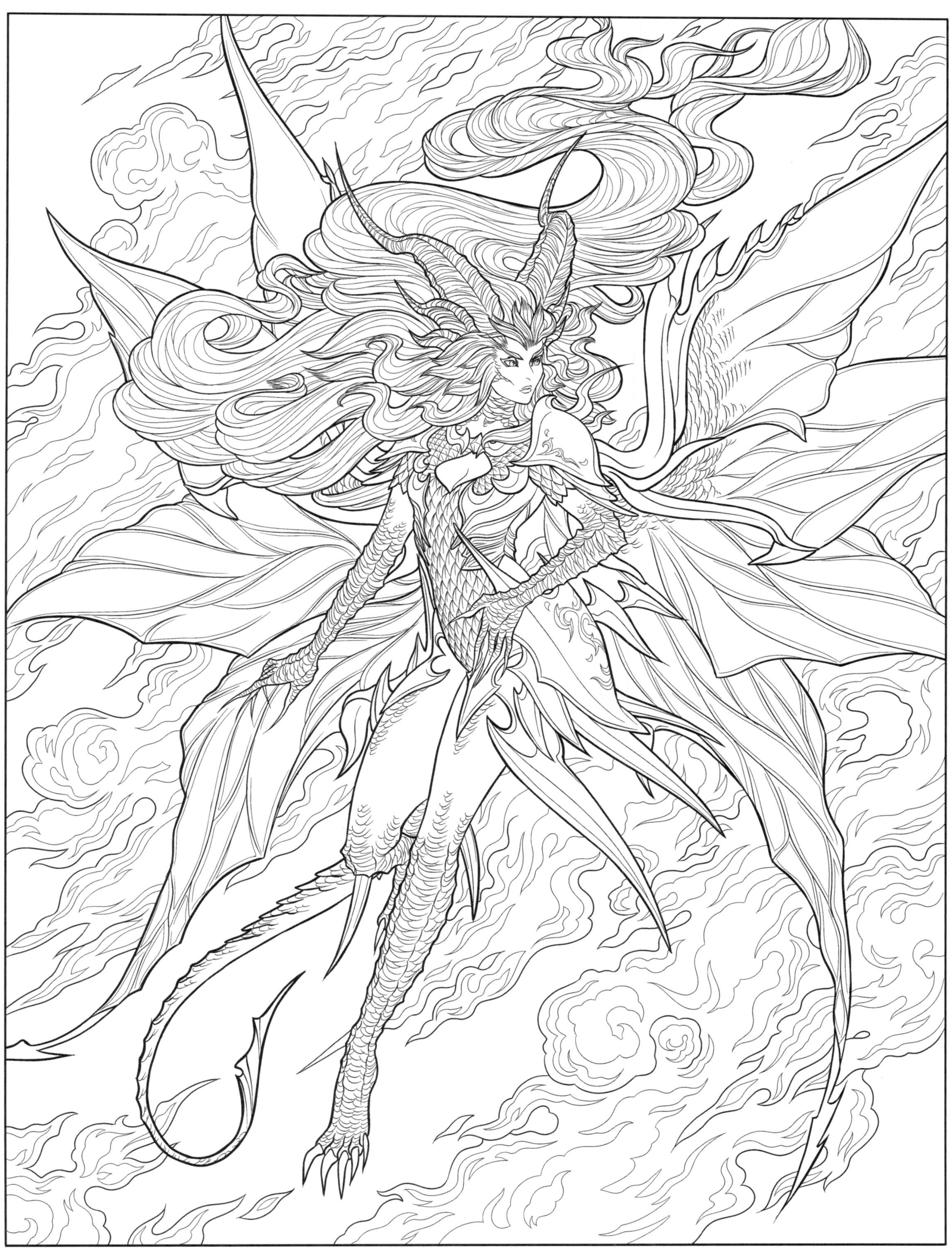

Mechanical Menace

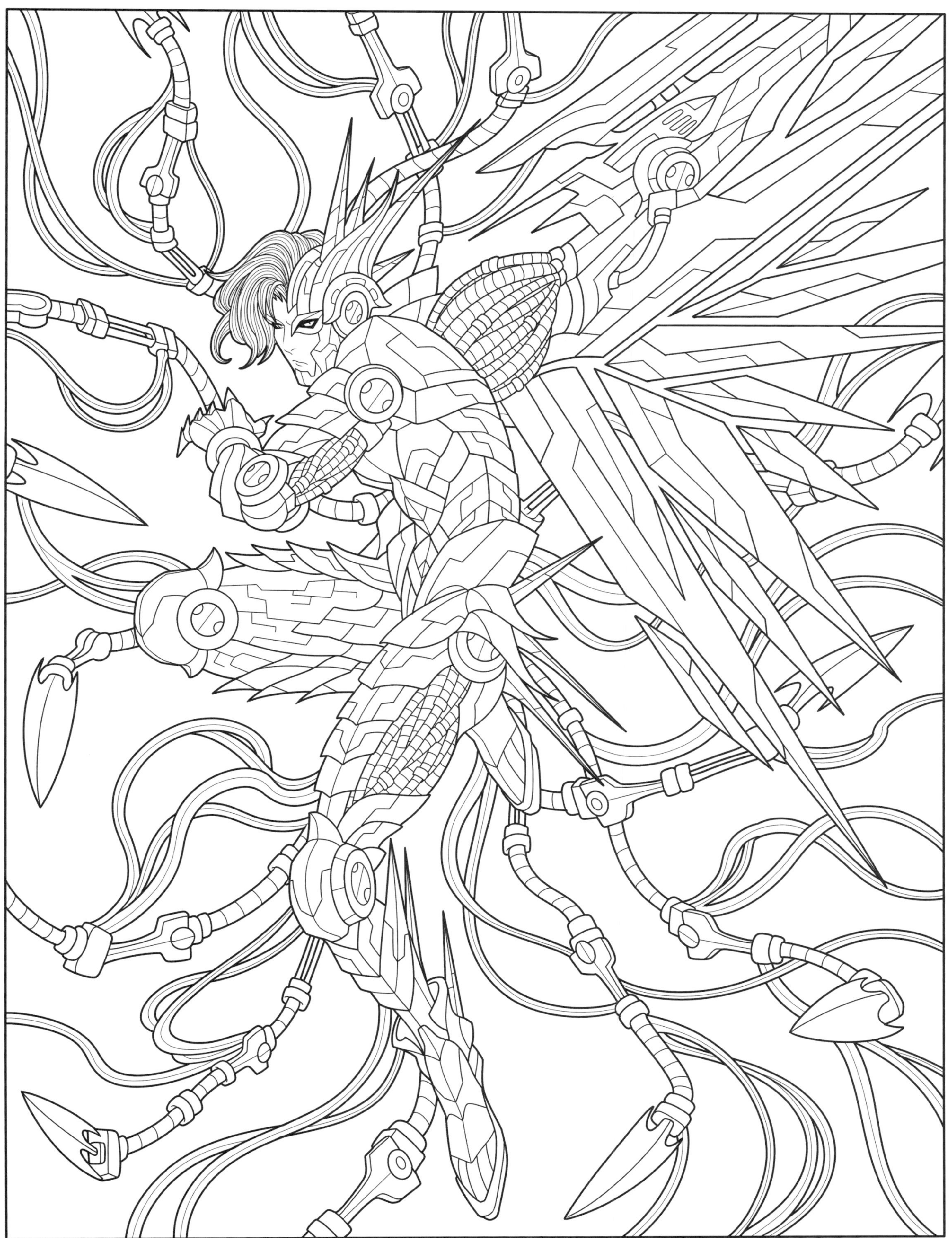

Ghost of the Graveyard

Gliding through the dead of night.

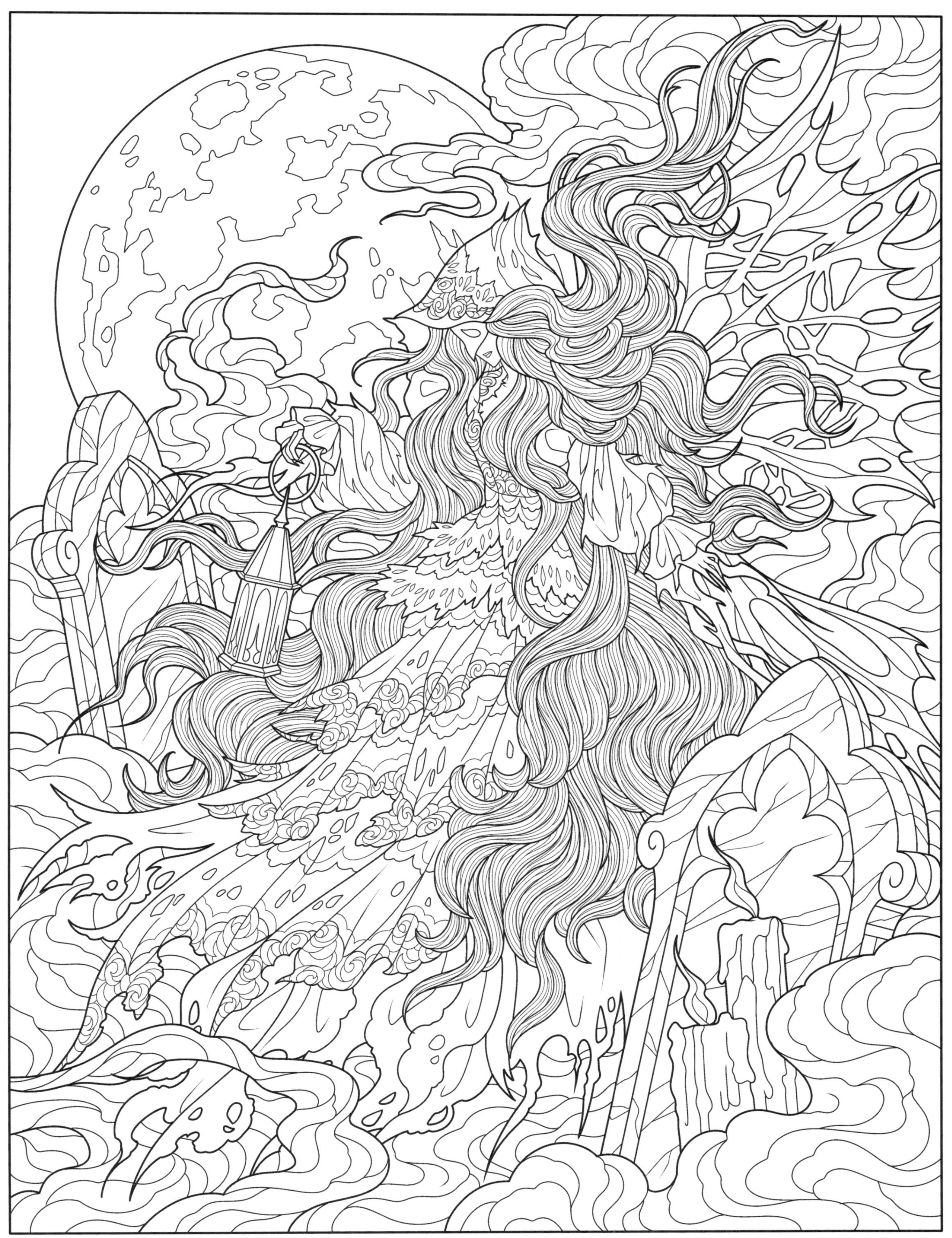

Demon of the Damned

Standing guard at the Gates of Hell.

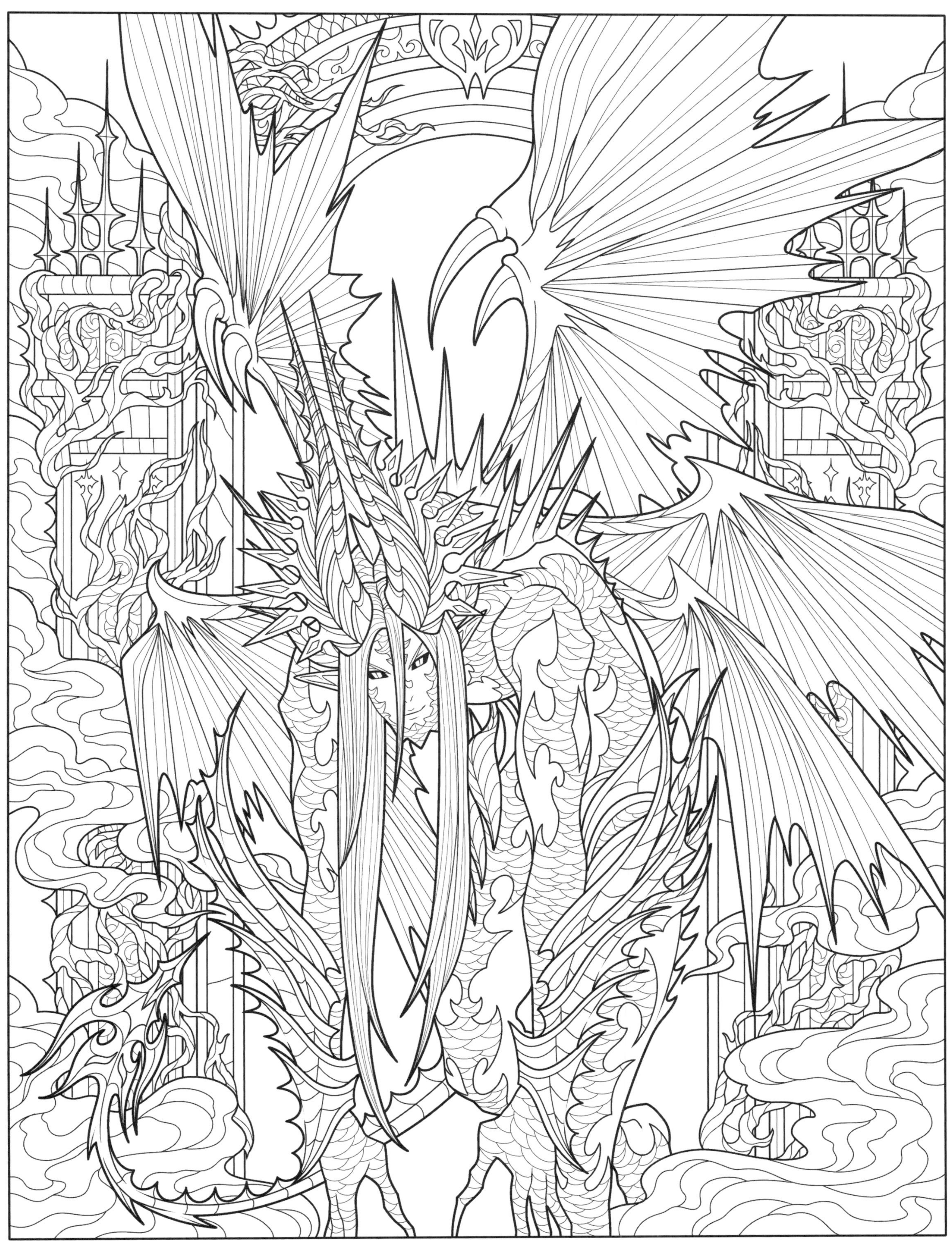

The Spider's Entrapment

Spinning a web of evil and entanglement.

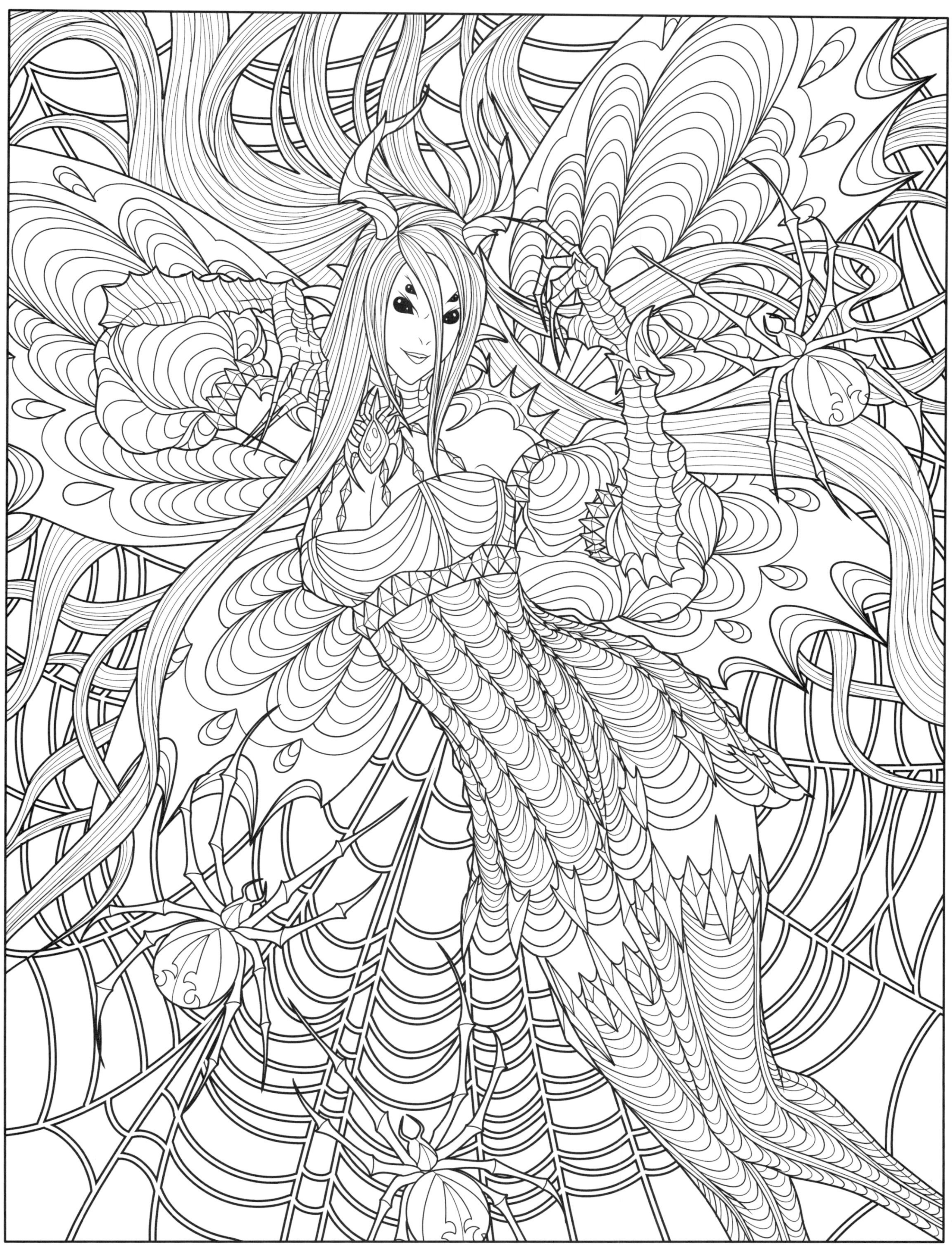

Serpent of the Sea

Creator of dark skies and stormy waters.

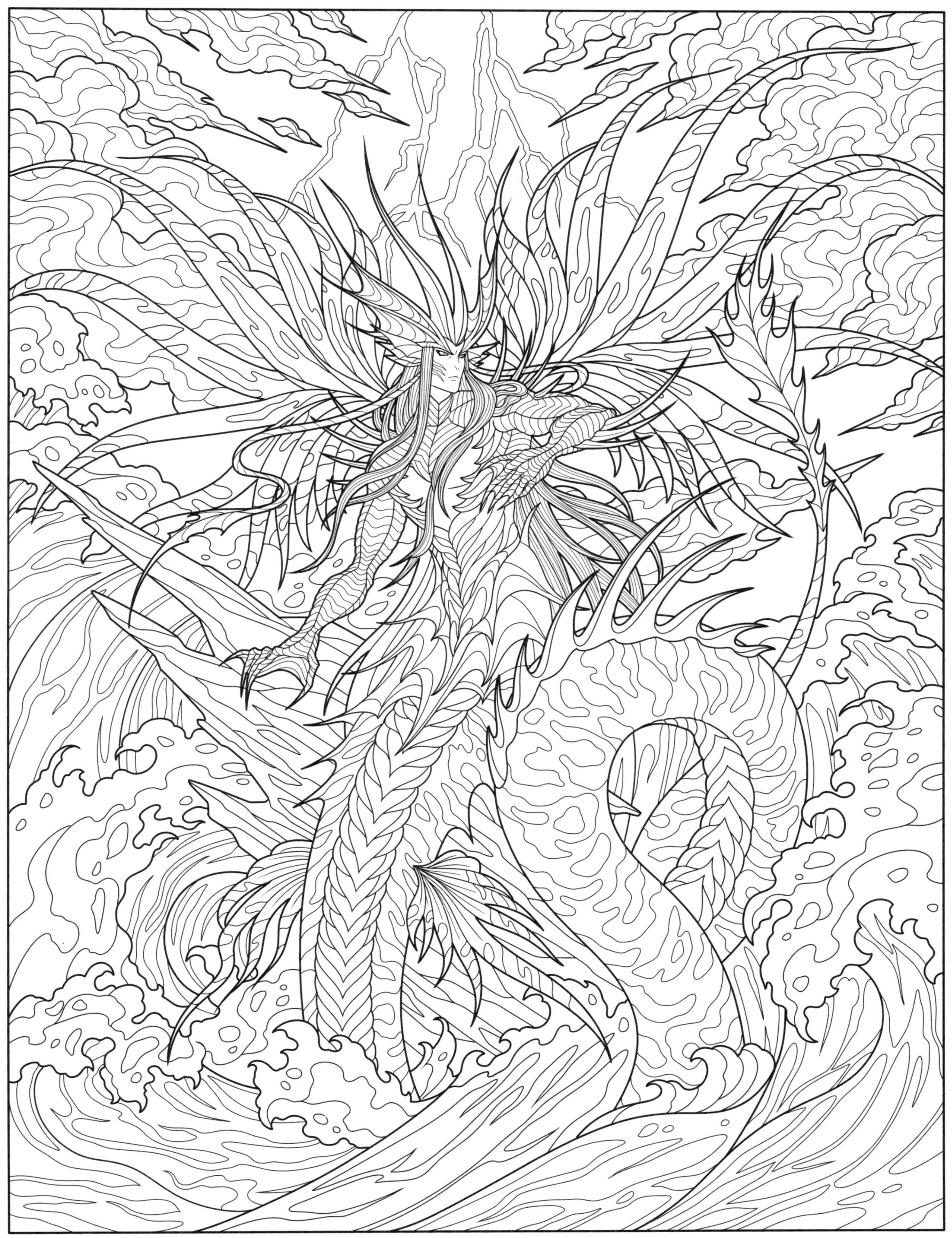

Fallen Angel

A deadly divine messenger cast out of Heaven.

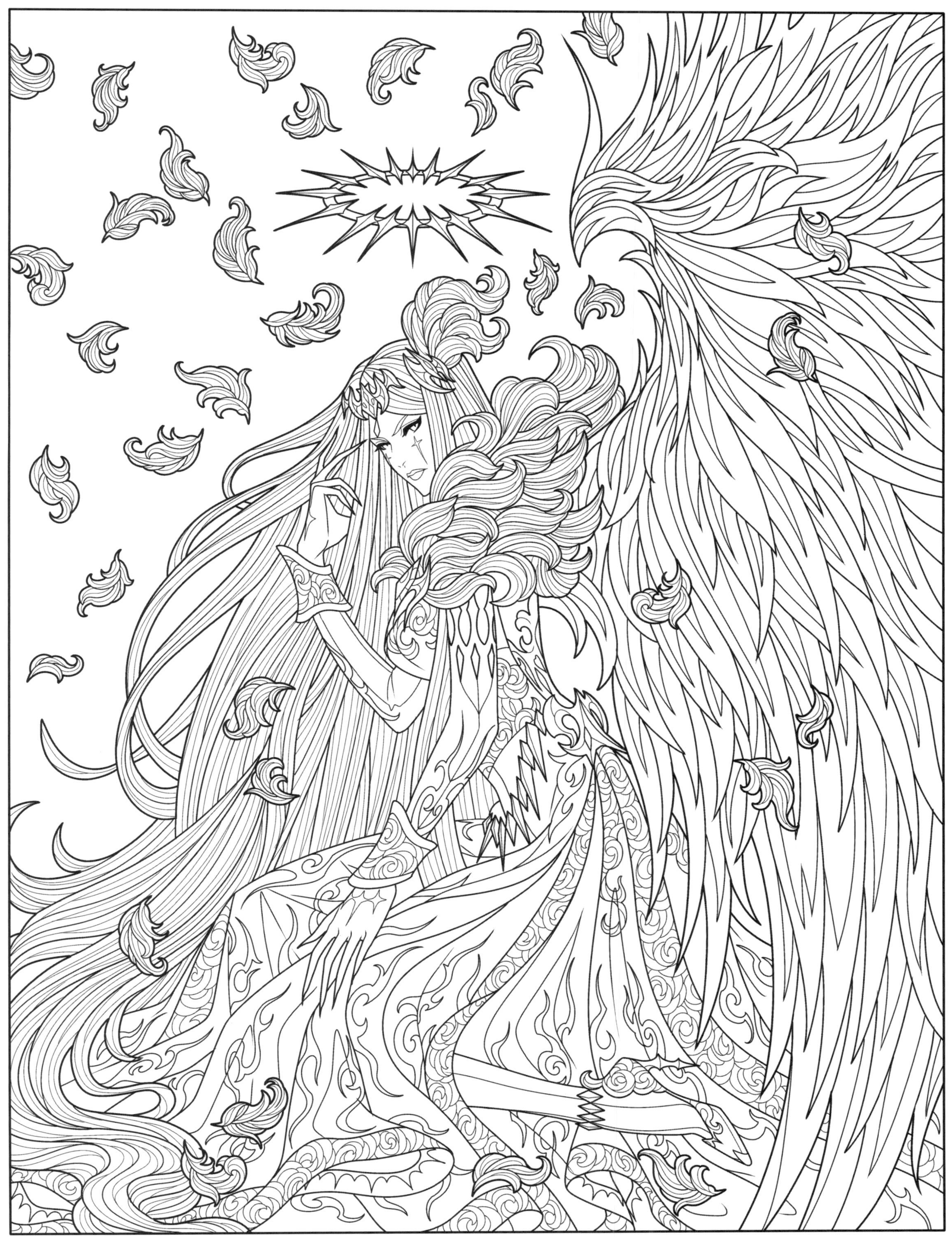

Skeletal Soul

Made of bones with spine-tingling senses.

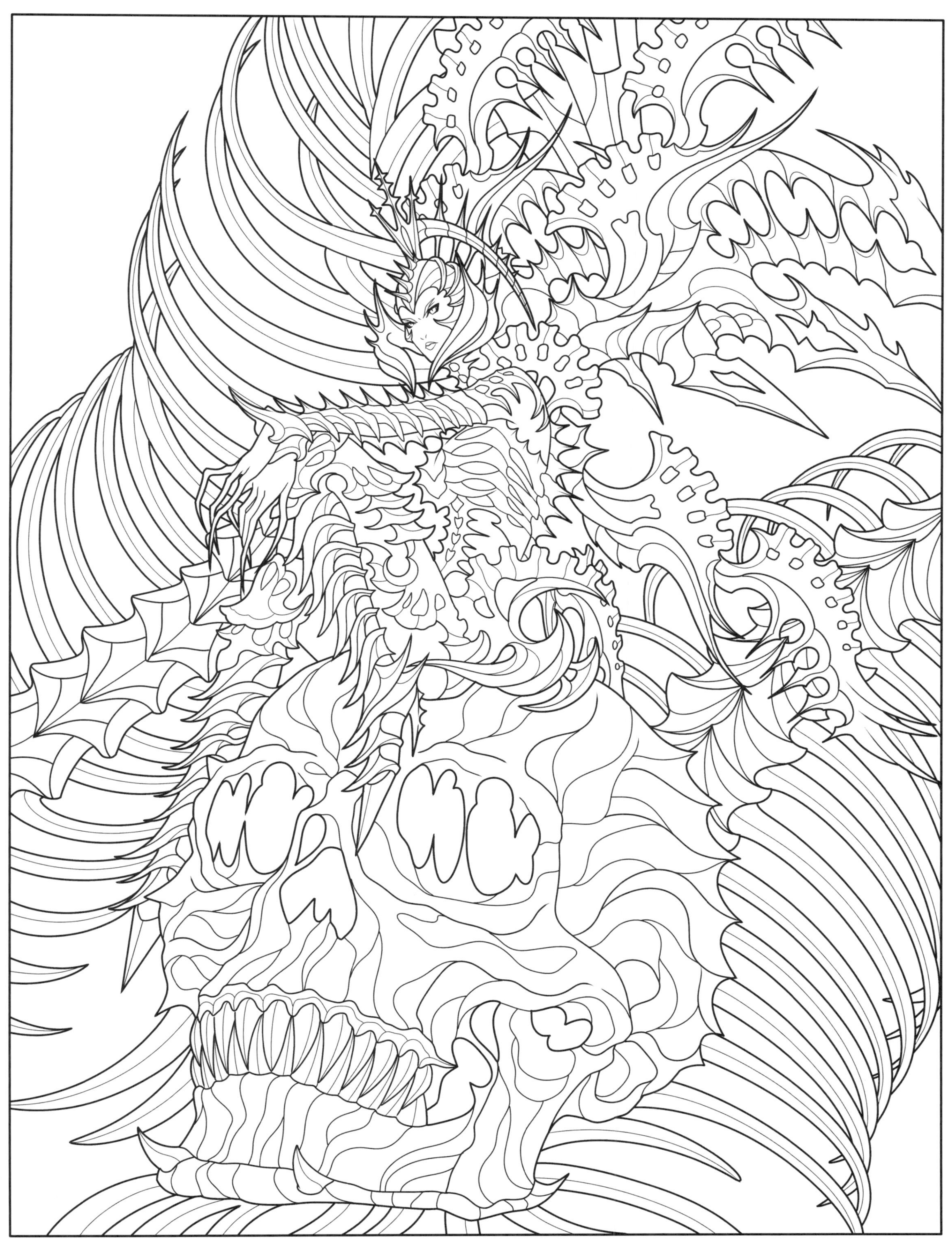

Sprite of the Swamp

Lurking in dark, poisonous waters.

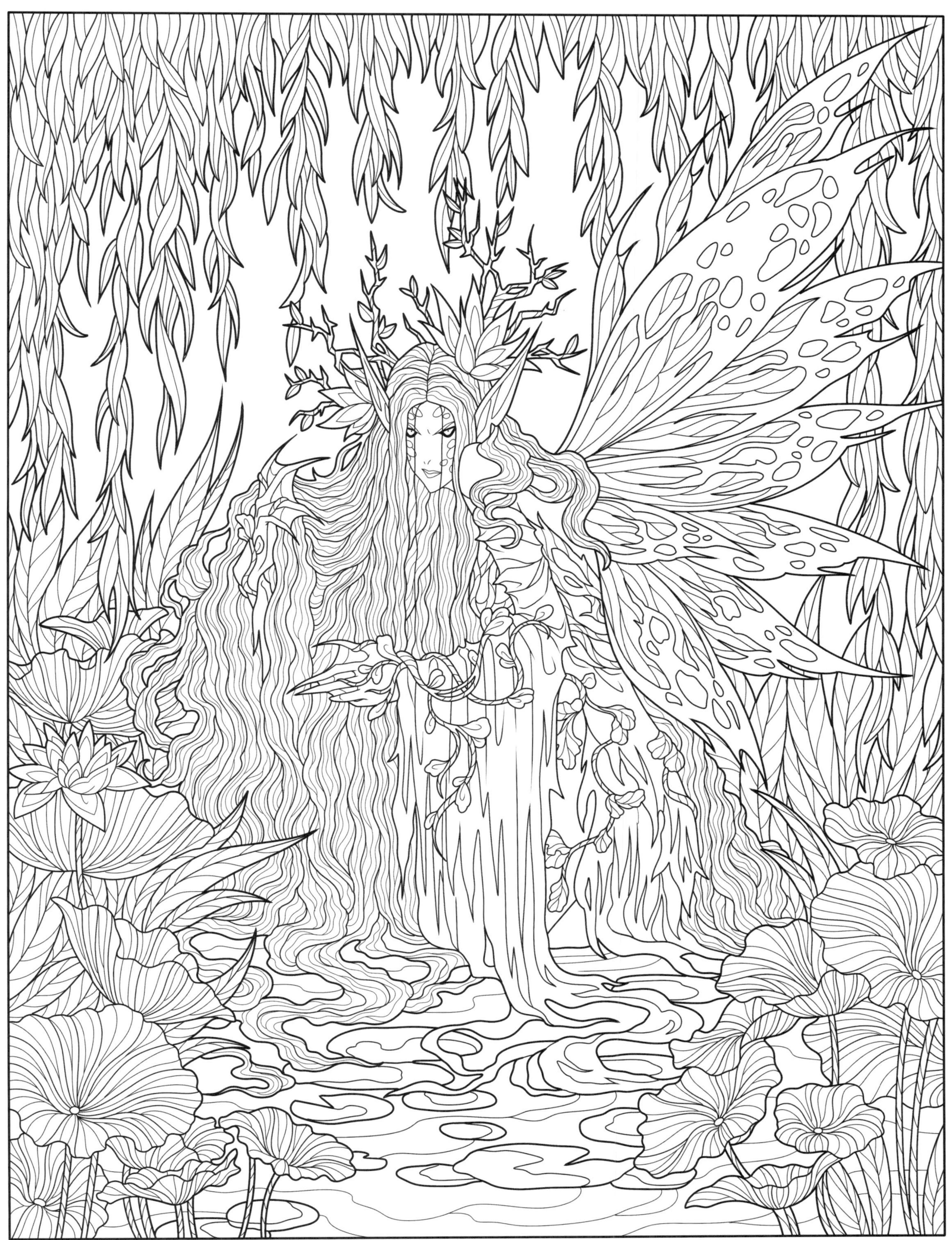

The Puppet Master

Manipulating the strings of fate.

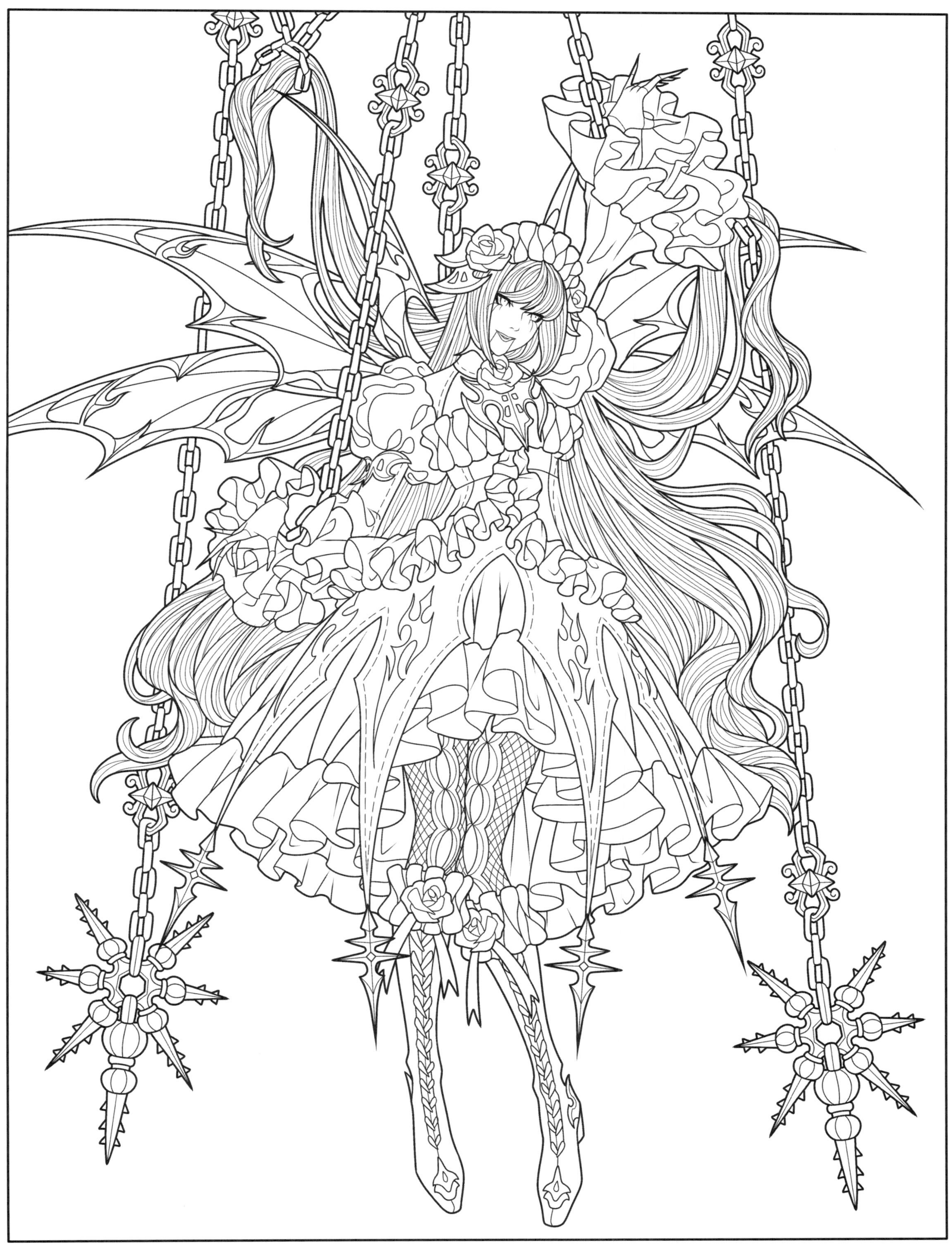

Gothic Gargoyle

A twisted monster looming over dark castles.

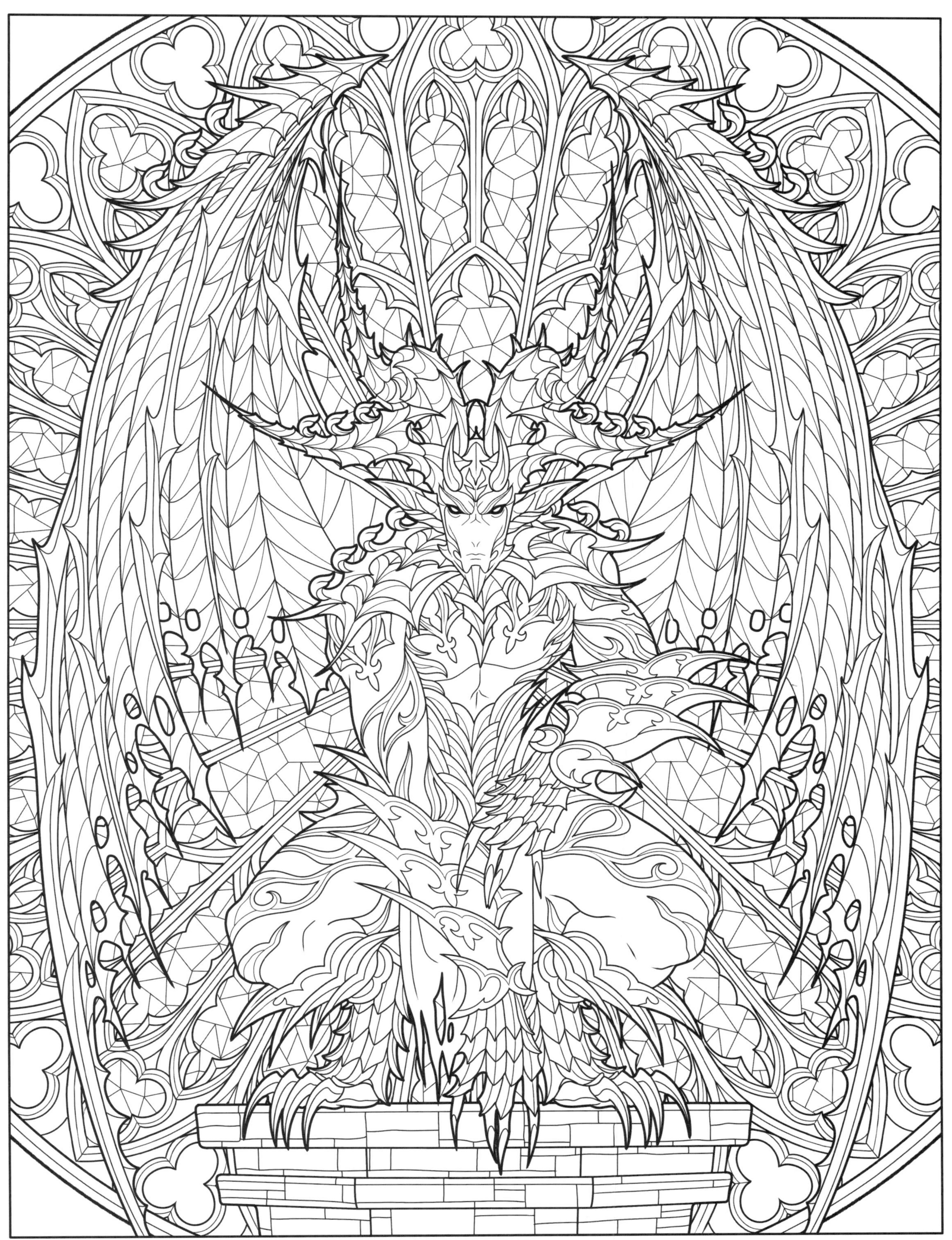

Peacock Power

Deadly extravagance in the eye of a feather.

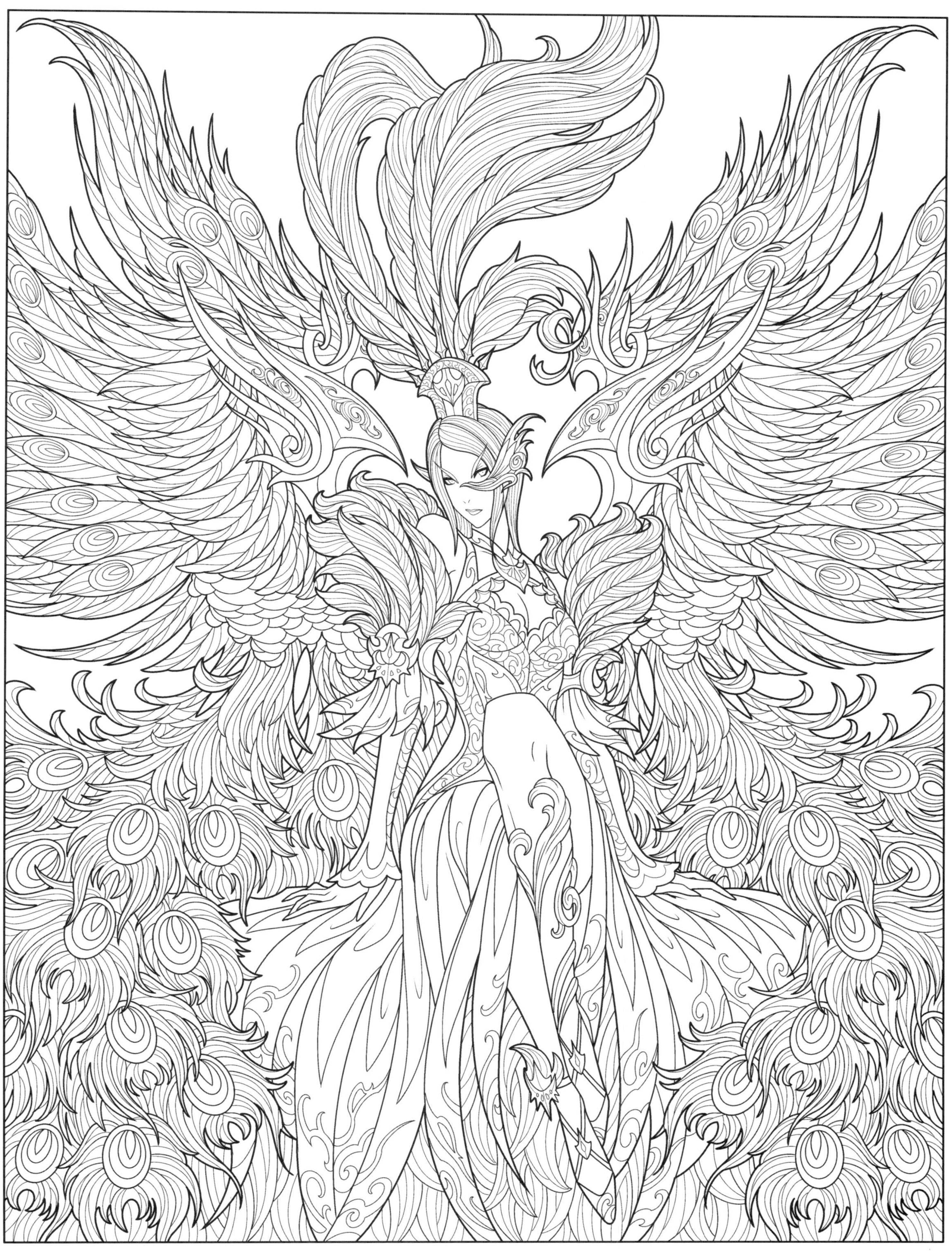

At the Masquerade Ball

Malice and mayhem in disguise.

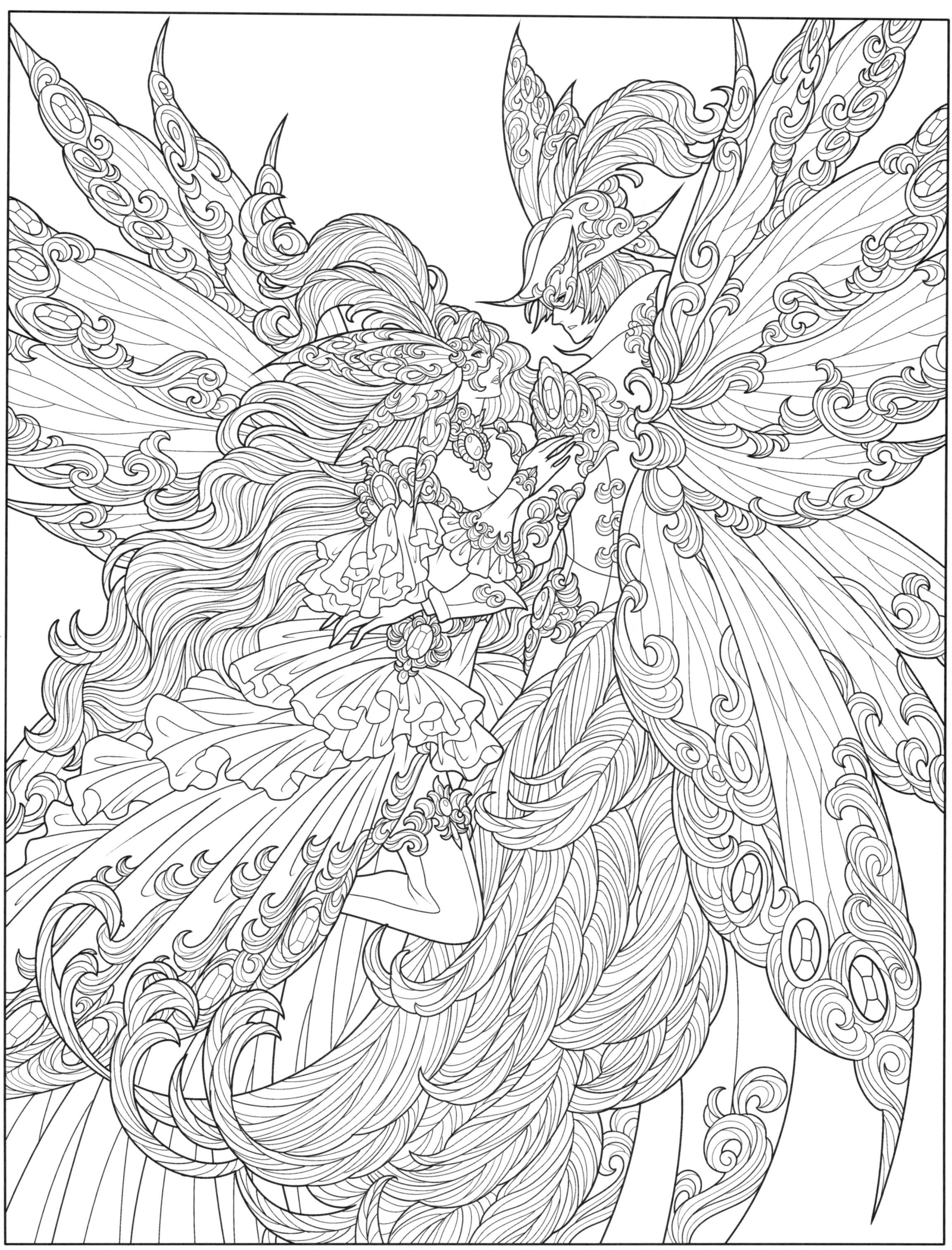

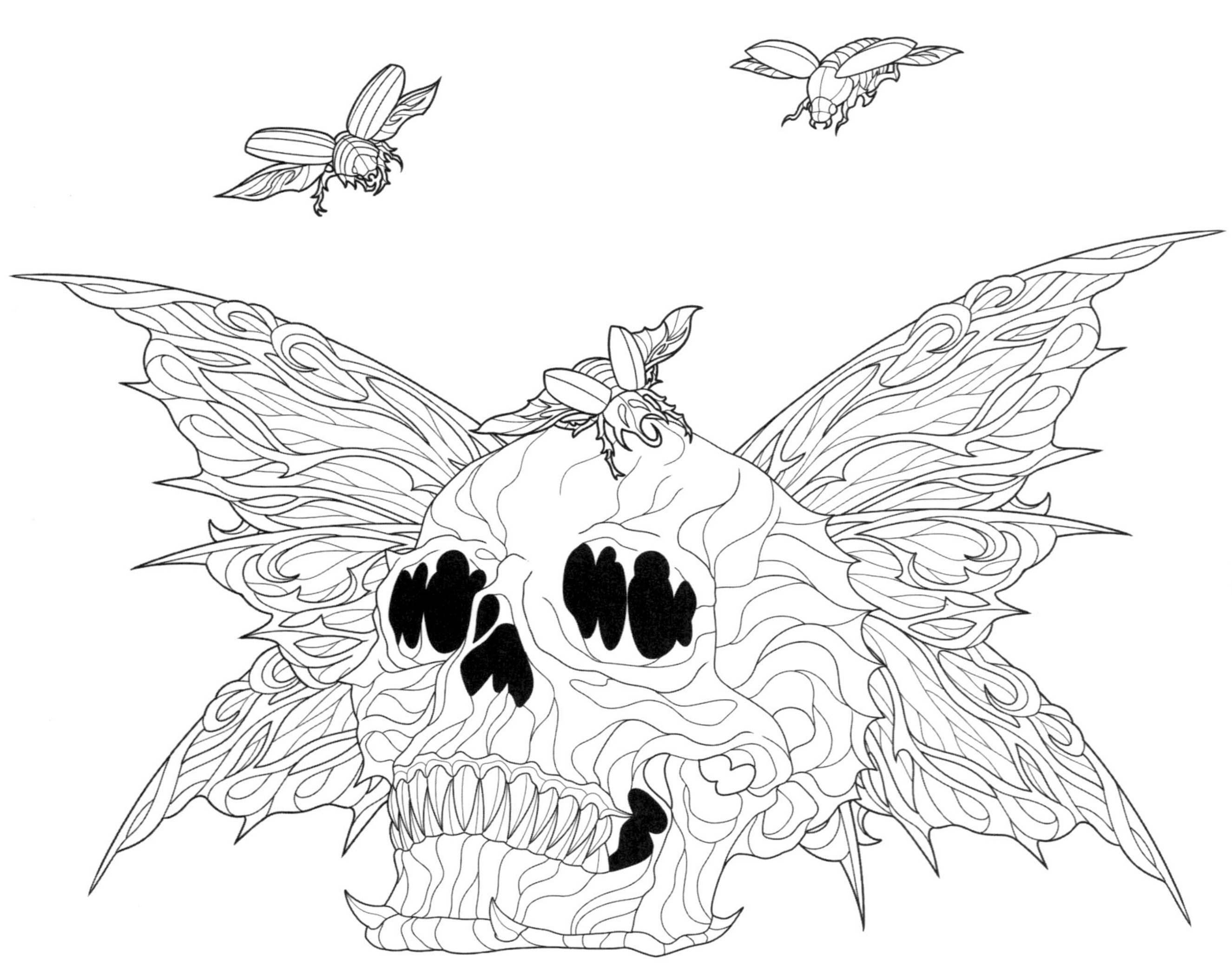